THE

ADVANTAGE

A SIMPLE A TO Z PLAYBOOK TO ACE YOUR INTERVIEWS AND BUILD YOUR DREAM CAREER

DR. FREDERICK SIDNEY CORREA
& FREDERICK SAVIO CORREA

INDIA • SINGAPORE • MALAYSIA

ISBN 979-8-89026-758-0

“Don’t Trust Luck, Learn to Earn”

— Late Frank Correa

Founder St. Jude’s Business Training Centre (Est. 1966)

This book is dedicated to our family.

All we need is us!

When we have each other,

We have everything.

Contents

Testimonials for Enhance Your Employability with Ikigai

The high level of early attrition seen among management trainees in Corporate India is an issue that has perplexed many of the stakeholders—corporate managers, academicians, business schools, etc. This early attrition has negatively impacted the industry and other stakeholders over the last decade and a half. Often the students and management trainees as a group end up taking the blame for wasting resources.

The authors have delved deep into this phenomenon and have conceptualized in a structured fashion what causes this early attrition and how professionals can prepare themselves for a fulfilling career. They bring together the role played by the business schools, industry interactions, the employer's organizational support to trainees, and the individual's awareness of self and interest in improving their employability in a fluid and straightforward fashion.

Management students significantly will gain enormously by using this approach and preparing themselves for a career of their interest and liking and living a fulfilling life.

Sundara Rajan, Founder Director, Thomas Assessments (India and SAARC)

In the various companies I have built and the thousands of corporations my team or I have consulted, one common element is a bane during the recruitment of graduates–"Employability."

There has been a lot of research on the concept of employability, yet many of us still suffer from the problem of finding employable graduates. Sometimes, the solution to a critical issue is on the shelf, but we don't pick up the book and seek the same.

What I like about this book is its focus on a critical problem that can help solve the career woes of many while referring to various research works that further validate what is being spoken about and doing so in a manner that speaks to the career seekers.

As the book says, let's ignite the spark.

Ashwin Srivastava, Co-founder of Great Manager Institute; Serial Entrepreneur, Investor, and Government Advisor

Parachutes and the mind both work well when they are open. This book is an excellent culmination of wisdom, which allows professionals to equip themselves with all the tools required for self-discovery and success in the workplace. A good read if you want a fast-paced career but a must-read if you want a fulfilling one.

Dr. N. Sambandam, Board of Management Studies, AICTE; Former Dean of NITTIE, GIM

We grow as individuals and professionals intuitively, but when you have a clear focus and a structured learning model, it always helps. As an SME on employability studies, Dr. Correa has partnered with 'Vans Skilling Advisory,' sharing his insights and the same passion for developing a unique 'lab in a box' concept to enhance the employability of business school graduates. His deep insights and Savio Correa's multi-decade experience in corporate training are unique and a thought-provoking amalgam. I recommend this book to all young and aspiring leaders!

Dr. Srinivas Chunduru, Founder, Vans Group (Vans Investments, Vans Skilling); Member of the Board—OSPL (OLA), Crowdera, AF Finance (Avail); Former CHRO Piramal Group, Executive Director Piramal Housing Finance

This book has found a gap in today's corporate environment and seeks to share solutions to overcome that gap. As a professional with over twenty years of working in the corporate world, I have always wondered about the vast gap in the India context between 'the real world' and what we are taught as students in business school. Most of what we learn isn't enough to make us successful in our careers, and each person is left to fend for themselves, and the onus to have a fulfilling career is an individual endeavor!

'Enhance Your Employability with Ikigai' is an eye-opener that helps illuminate this existing blind spot. The book focusses on simple and practical suggestions for those who are either new management students who join the corporate world with great dreams and ambitions of growing into business honchos during their respective careers or even existing professionals who wish that their learning isn't through trial and error. Thanks to this book, whether a fresh management graduate or an experienced professional, the reader will be better prepared for corporate life and hopefully find their purpose.

Cecilia Azavedo Global Head of HR Business Partners, Biocon Biologics; Former Head of Human Resources, Johnson & Johnson (Janssen India), Merk Group,

Learning in its true sense requires guidance, attention, and individual effort. This book provides a roadmap for the same. It is simple in its presentation and content. The author's universal and strategic approach can guide any young manager's quest for success. It is a contemporary ready reckoner for all management students and professionals of today seeking an alignment of their purpose and corporate career choices. A must-read indeed!

Aparna Sharma, Author, Between 'U & Me' and Reality Bytes—The Role of HR in Today's World; Independent Director, Rajratan Global wire & T. S. Alloy (100% Tata Subsidiary); NHRD National Executive Board; Former Country Head, HR Lafarge

A very practical approach to explain the linkages between Ikigai and how to be organization ready at an early stage of your life. The authors use a game-changing approach of connecting the dots to help you achieve a clear career goal and address the big challenge of career dissatisfaction that could set in at a later stage for anybody.

Atulaya Goswami, UPL Limited, HR Head, India; China Fortune Land Development Ltd., Procter & Gamble

Crisp, practical, contemporary, and amazing. I commend the authors for articulating such a complex issue in such a compelling manner. This book will serve as an initiation guide for management students, aspiring management professionals, and young managers. It will also become a guiding principle and torchbearer for management and leadership to build a strategy around it. Easy value-adding read, highly recommended!

Ashish Gakrey, Founder HR shapers; HR Leader Capgemini; Teleperformance, Loop Mobile, Zycus

I have known Mr. Savio Correa for almost a decade during our various interactions at training forums. His unique storytelling style is both entertaining and relatable across age groups. This book is a wonderful collection of years of experience packed into wisdom insights for the youth making career decisions. It does not theorize. Instead focuses on the real problems of the urban youth and proposes tangible solutions, a must-read for all young professionals striving to make a mark in the corporate world.

Sneha Jain Paul, HR Head, Bazaar Kolkata; Former Head of HR for Manyavar, Wacker Chemie

Dr. Correa has been a part of our board of studies and has contributed significantly to shaping the curriculum and pedagogy in line with industry requirements. What amazes me is the depth of his knowledge and his ability to connect with his audience. I am not surprised to see the ease with which the authors have been able to articulate such a complex subject in such a compelling manner. A must-read!

Seema Saini, CEO of N. L. Dalmia Educational Society

Advance Praise for The Ikigai Advantage

Brilliantly practical and incredibly insightful, this interview playbook is a game-changer for anyone looking to master the art of interviewing. With a wealth of valuable tips and strategies, it provides a comprehensive roadmap for navigating every stage of the interview process with confidence and ease. Whether you're a seasoned professional or just starting out in your career, this playbook is an invaluable resource that will help you land your dream job and achieve your career goals. Highly recommended!

Sandeep Batra, Partner, Sapphire Human Solutions Private Limited; Former President, YES Bank; Ex-HSBC; Ex-Bank of America

This interview playbook is a true masterpiece that should be on every job seeker's bookshelf. The author's deep understanding of the hiring process is evident throughout the playbook, which offers a comprehensive, practical guide to acing your job interviews. The playbook is packed with expert advice, real-world examples, and step-by-step guidance that will help you confidently navigate any interview scenario. Whether you're a seasoned professional or just starting out, this playbook is an essential tool that will help you stand out from the competition and land your dream job.

Raj Sakpal, TA Lead-Lower Gulf & Europe, Digital bank; Former TA Lead: Asia pacific, Clariant; Ex-Kornferry; Ex-Mondelez

I must congratulate the authors for addressing a major gap for candidate preparation before the interview round that will greatly enhance the chances of cracking the interview as the candidate will be better prepared to present himself/herself in a more comprehensive way. Thoughts will be more aligned and answers will be more crisp and sharp. Being part of the recruitment industry for the last 20 years, I have seen numerous candidates who can present themselves very well when the question is directed towards KRAs and accomplishments, but open ended questions are where they flounder the most.

This book will be a must have for all recruitment/search firms and should be part of the training manual for candidate preparation. It will add tremendous value and enhance candidate experience. Even if the candidate is not able to clear the interview round, learning which he/ she will get post reading the book and preparation, will help them understand themselves better and sharpen their loose ends.

For the corporations/client companies, this will help them standardise their interview process and can make it far more organised as we have observed this a lot of times, even Senior professionals/line managers, when it comes to interviewing candidates, sometimes they are not able to conduct the interview in a more meaningful manner as they are not well prepared.

Mayank Chandra, Managing Partner, Antal International Network; Former Partner, Adecco People One

This interview playbook is a game-changer for anyone looking to ace their job interviews. The author's expertise in the field is evident throughout the playbook, which offers a comprehensive approach to interview preparation and execution. The playbook is packed with practical tips, expert advice, and real-world examples that will help you confidently navigate any interview scenario. Whether you're a job seeker or a seasoned professional, this playbook is an invaluable resource that will help you land your dream job.

Anand Talwar, Partner, Petram Consultants; Former CHRO, ITC InfoTech; Former HR Head Reliance Telecom

The Ikigai Advantage is a game-changing resource that empowers job seekers to confidently navigate the complex world of interviews. With practical tips, proven strategies, and an emphasis on personal branding, this playbook is a transformative journey that will boost your confidence and increase your chances of landing your dream job. Invest in this indispensable resource and unlock your true potential in interviews.

Furthermore, this playbook addresses the most common interview pitfalls and offers practical solutions to overcome them. Whether it's dealing with nerves, tackling tough questions, or negotiating salary, you'll find expert guidance to handle any challenge that comes your way.

Nikita Aneja, Head HR, Viacom18; Former Manager- Talent Management and Campus Relations Edelweiss Financial Services; Former Lead Campus Recruitment, Tata Motors

I have read and had the golden opportunity to launch the first book by the authors - 'Enhance your employability with Ikigai'.

As a book lover and someone who keenly observes the writing styles of authors, I must admit that this author duo's style is a workbook style of writing.

They make the reader feel easy and unintimidated with concepts.

I see the same style repeating in this new book. The Ikigai Advantage is a deep delve into areas that can surely help aspiring professionals to reach their goals if the tools and techniques are deployed.

This book is a workbook for anyone to just blindly apply and leave it to the mechanics to do it's magic.

K Rajeev Narayan, CEO, The Leadership Elements India (The only book based leadership consulting house in APAC & UAE); Former Head of L&D, TVS Motors; Former Senior Leadership Coach & Facilitator, Dale Carnegie Training Institute

The Ikigai Advantage is an essential resource in the complex and competitive modern job market. The authors present a detailed plan for succeeding in interviews and finding success in one's chosen field by using the Japanese idea of 'Ikigai,' which describes the moment when one's "passion, talent, and the needs of the world all come together." The authors' goal in writing this book was to make the process of preparing for an interview feel less challenging and more like an opportunity for growth. It goes beyond simply finding employment by encouraging you to pursue a line of work that is in harmony with your Ikigai. I hope that you find the information in this book helpful in navigating the modern job market and that it also motivates you to create and pursue a meaningful professional path. This is a much awaited sequel to their earlier book "Enhance your Employability with Ikigai".

Dr. Amit Mittal, Pro Vice Chancellor (Research), Chitkara University Chandigarh; Former Dean (Management), Chitkara University Chandigarh.

As you pursue your career goals, THE IGIKAI ADVANTAGE will be your trusted guide to unlocking the secrets to interview success.

If you want to stand out from the competition and leave a lasting impression on your interviewer, this is the only book you need. It is the ultimate secret weapon you have been searching for. Frederick has designed this book to equip you with the necessary skills to master the art of interviewing and land your ideal job through its comprehensive approach, expert advice, and real-world examples.

This book contains valuable insights, practical advice, and step-by-step instructions. It is meticulously designed to equip you with the confidence and knowledge required to navigate any interview scenario confidently. This playbook is an indispensable resource that will propel you to new heights and elevate your professional voyage, whether you are an experienced professional or just beginning your career.

Dr. Ankita Singh, Senior Vice President and Global HR Head, CIGNEX; Founder, HR Association of India

Authors' Note

Congratulations on making it to the interview stage of your job search. We know how much effort goes into creating a winning CV and cover letter; the last thing you want is to fail your interview. Making the most of this opportunity is essential, as only around 5% of applicants earn an interview from a pool of hundreds. Relaxing at this stage could mean missing out on the job you want.

Thorough preparation is essential to succeed in the interview. The interviewer expects nothing but the best candidate for the role, and a comprehensive prep includes understanding the "why" of a question and the "how" of answering it. While you may not be asked these exact questions in precisely these words, having answer maps in mind will help you prepare for just about anything the interviewer throws your way.

This book has the A to Z interview questions you may encounter, strategies on constructing your answers, and over 500 sample answers which will help you develop your perfect interview pigeonhole according to your personality. So, let's start crafting compelling stories that showcase your experiences, skills, and values in a way that resonates with the interviewer, with purpose and authenticity, to land that dream job!

"The best way to appreciate your job is to imagine yourself without one."

Building Your Pigeonhole Strategy

Many job seekers are constantly surprised by how unprepared they are. These professionals tell me that many inexperienced job seekers feel they can wing it and that most are usually tongue-tied with the most straightforward questions, which they should know are coming.

You may have mailed a brilliant CV and cover letter. You may be wearing the perfect clothes on the day of the interview. But you are not getting hired if you can't convince the interviewer face to face that you are the right person for the job.

Many candidates hesitate after the first open-ended question, stumble and stutter through a disjointed litany of CV sound bites. Other interviewees gave canned answers that only highlighted their memory skills.

For example, the most common job interview question: Tell me about yourself, hit job seekers like a stun gun. A typical candidate frantically searches their brain for the answer to this seemingly innocuous question. This common interview question is not at all innocuous. This question can make or break a job interview. As an applicant, you should consider this question a great opportunity to sell yourself to a prospective employer. This opportunity may be the only time you can talk freely during the job-hunting process, uncovering many things that make you uniquely qualified.

Unfortunately, most candidates wind up hemming and hawing and growing increasingly nervous until they knock a chair over on the way out.

So, tell me, who are you?

The success or failure of many interviews will depend on your ability to answer this simple question. The interview process is a type of sale. In this case, you are the product and the seller. If you are not ready to discuss your specific features and benefits, you will unlikely motivate an interviewer to buy this product. Most candidates don't have the answer to direct questions like, How would you describe yourself? Or, more simply, Who are you? They don't know the answer because they never thought about this question. Most people are uncomfortable with introspection.

However, it is necessary to take time now to get to know yourself better. You may have passed through school with flying colors, but you will spiral out of the job market unless you take the time to perform a personal inventory. There are selfish reasons why you should do this. During your lifetime, you will work approximately 60,000 hours. Whether that work is productive and fulfilling will depend to a large extent on how well you have identified and utilized your dominant skills and talents right from the start. Match your skills and talents with the right industry, job, and company, and your work life will be successful and happy. You remain frustrated, unhappy, and apathetic if you do not do this. Given an option, I recommend the former!

Information at your fingertips

Have you put together a resume? Of course, you have. Okay, that process should provide you with all the information you need to answer the question, Who are you? , in a way that will knock the interviewer's socks off. Most candidates write a resume together as if it were just a catalog of their achievements and education. A resume or a CV should also reflect the 'real you' behind the facts and dates. You should see your resume process as an opportunity to examine the qualities that make you unique and that you want to improve. This exercise is an opportunity to organize information about your education, jobs, and volunteer activities.

You must gather all the following information. Having separate folders with relevant data, citations, notes, and more is an excellent idea. Your employment history produces a separate sheet for every full-time and part-time job, regardless of tenure. Yes, even summer jobs are essential: they demonstrate resourcefulness, responsibility, and initiative, and you are already developing a sense of independence while living with your parents. Whether you want to include some, all, or none of these short-term jobs on your CV or discuss them during your interview is a decision you will make later. For now, write everything about every task.

For each employer, this includes:

- Company name, address, telephone number, and e-mail address
- Names of all your supervisors and, whenever possible, where or how their contact details
- Letters of recommendation
- Exact dates (months and years) you have planned. For each task, including specific duties and responsibilities
- Supervisory experience (the number of people you manage).
- Specific skills required for the job
- Major achievements
- The dates you got promoted
- Any award, honour, and special recognition you have received
- For each part-time job, include the hours you worked per week
- Responsibilities: Write one or two sentences observing the tasks you have handled in each position you conducted
- Use numbers as often as possible to demonstrate the scope of your responsibilities
- Skills: Name the specific skills needed to perform your duties—highlighting those you have developed on the job
- Significant achievements: This is the place to brag. But be sure to back up each achievement with nuances, including results

Your volunteer activities

The fact that you did not get paid for a specific job, such as filling envelopes for a local political candidate, running a car wash to raise money for people experiencing homelessness, or operating a drug hotline, is no reason to leave it off your resume. Having hired hundreds of people during my career, I assure you that many interviewers will consider and weigh your after-hours activities. Workaholics rarely make the best employees.

Your educational accomplishments

If you are a recent college graduate or are still in college, you do not need to re-read your high school experiences. Even if you have a bachelor's degree or are a graduate student, you should list both graduate and undergraduate work.

Your extracurricular activities

I am always interested and am impressed by the candidates who talk about the books they read and the activities they enjoy. So, list all the sports, clubs, and other activities you participated in or outside the school. Each activity, club, or group must include the following:

Name and purpose

- Any office held by you; Special committees formed, chaired, or attended by you; the specific situation you played
- Duties and responsibilities of each role
- Major achievements
- The honours and awards that you have received. Include the ones you have received from school(s), community groups, church groups, clubs, and the like. If you are out of graduate school or college for a long time, you can still include awards from prestigious high schools (prep schools or professional schools).

You need to dig deeper

Once you complete these forms, you will see a lot of information on them. But they all tell you about what you have done and where you are. These facts alone will not give you a job. It would help if you took some time to think about your personal history so that you are prepared to present the 'real you' during the interview. Use the following questions as a guide:

1. Which achievements did you like the most? What are you proud of? (Be prepared to tell the interviewer how these achievements relate to the situation.)

2. What mistakes have you made? Why did they happen? How have you learned from them?

3. How well do you interact with the authorities, teachers, and parents?

4. What are your favorite sports and games? Think about how you play these games and what they say about you. Are you highly competitive? Do you give up very quickly? Are you a good loser or a bad winner?

5. What kind of people are your friends? Do you only connect with people who are very similar to you? Do you enjoy differences in others or only tolerate them? What are the things that have caused your friendship to end? What does this say about you?

6. If you ask a group of friends and acquaintances to describe you, which adjective will they use? List them all, good and bad. Why would people describe you like this? Are there specific behaviors, skills, achievements, or failures that make you recognize others in the eyes? What are they? This exercise will be most effective if you write your answers. Because it is only for your eyes, you should not be concerned about the creation of beautiful prose, or for that matter, even complete sentences. The only important thing is honesty.

Paint the complete picture

Now, look at all those you have written so far and distribute them in multiple lists with the following headings:

- My strongest skills
- Areas in which I am most knowledgeable
- The strongest parts of my personality
- Things I do best
- Skills that I must develop to do well in my career
- Aspects of my personality I could stand to improve

If you take the time to do this exercise honestly and thoroughly, you will be amazed at the results. This exercise should help you feel things you never knew about yourself more accurately. I urge you to engage in this self-testing process, even if there is no imminent need to use the information. Then, when you set up your interview, make your lists, along with another clean sheet of paper, and answer the following questions:

1. What would explain to this employer on my list that I deserve the position I am interviewing for?
2. What strengths, achievements, skills, and areas of knowledge make me most qualified for this position?
3. What weaknesses should I admit to, if asked about them, and how will I indicate that I have improved or will improve them?

As you traverse this journey, you will encounter other common interview questions, strategies for constructing your answers, and sample answers to help you develop your pigeonhole strategy to steer the interview from the driver's seat.

"Don't be afraid to fail. Don't waste energy trying to cover up failure. Learn from your failures and go on to the next challenge."

A 1 Tell Me About Yourself

There are plenty of times when you'll hear these exact words: Tell me about yourself. Interviewers might have their versions that are asking pretty much the same thing, including

- I have your resume before me, but tell me more about yourself.
- Could you walk me through your resume?
- I'd love to hear more about your journey.
- Tell me a little bit more about your background.

This little gem usually crops up as an ice-breaker at the start of the interview. Describing yourself will help the interviewer determine if you fit the company's work culture and are a good fit for the position. What you think about yourself creates a first impression of your personality. The recruiter seeks honesty, so be straightforward with your answers. Declare your achievements, unique strengths, and likes and dislikes but avoid sensitive topics. Be cautious not to give unnecessary personal details about yourself. Keep it short, relevant, and professional; this isn't the time to talk about your family and hobbies unless you know something particular about the company that would lead you to believe otherwise.

Whatever you do, don't waste this time. Everyone has a different approach; keep it to 30 seconds or less, while others will say you should aim for a minute or talk for no more than two minutes.

A first impression can color the rest of the interview. Most decisions to reject a candidate are taken in the first few minutes, including your greeting, handshake, eye contact, and the first thing you say, which may very well be your response to Tell me about yourself.

Direct your response to the question;

a. Talk about who you are professionally
b. Highlight your competencies
c. Talk about why you are here.

Sample 1

Here's a sample response that addresses all three points

a. I am a highly motivated and experienced professional in the field of marketing. Over the past eight years, I've worked with various clients across various industries, giving me a broad perspective on marketing strategies and tactics.
b. My competencies lie in my ability to think strategically and creatively, develop comprehensive marketing plans, and execute them to achieve measurable results. I am also skilled in digital marketing, including SEO, PPC, and social media advertising. Additionally, I possess strong communication and interpersonal skills, allowing me to collaborate effectively with team members, clients, and stakeholders.
c. I am here because I am excited to work with your company and contribute to your marketing efforts. I have been following your company for some time now and have been impressed with the innovative and impactful work that you have been doing. I am confident that my skills and experience can help take your marketing efforts to the next level and achieve even greater success. I am excited about possibly joining your team and working towards a common goal.

Sample 2

I am an innovative customer service manager with six years of experience managing and monitoring all aspects of the customer service function, from solving customer problems to ensuring customer retention to increasing sales. (Who you are)

I have spent six years developing my skills as a customer service manager. I have attracted recognition and several awards, even national awards, three times. I love solving customer problems and overseeing my team members to do so too. (Competence highlights)

Even if I love my current position, I know that I am ready to take up a more challenging role in customer service, and that is why I am very excited about this position. (Why you are here).

Sample 3

a. Thank you for asking. Professionally, I am a marketing professional with over five years of experience in developing and executing successful marketing strategies across various industries. I have a Bachelor's degree in Marketing and a keen eye for consumer behavior, which has helped me to stay on top of market trends and adjust my approach accordingly.

b. Regarding competencies, I am a skilled communicator and problem solver. I have experience working with cross-functional teams to achieve objectives and am comfortable presenting complex ideas to technical and non-technical audiences. I am also proficient in using analytics to measure the effectiveness of marketing campaigns and make data-driven decisions.

c. I am here today because I am excited about working with a dynamic team in a growing industry. I have followed the company's success and am impressed by its commitment to innovation and excellence. I am confident that my skills and experience align with the position's needs and can contribute to the company's continued success.

Sample 4

I am a creative thinker who enjoys exploring alternative solutions to problems. My optimistic nature has helped me to persevere through tough times, and I never give up, no matter how difficult the situation is. However, I am not unrealistic and understand the importance of drawing a line between what is possible and what is not, and I accordingly take action.

My colleagues would describe me as a great team player, as I always prioritize the team's interests first. I have also facilitated team bonding through various team-building activities. I would easily fit in with your work culture based on these qualities.

Sample 5

Sure! So I've always enjoyed writing and public speaking, which led me to pursue writing-related passions. For example, I was an editor for our school newspaper in college. In addition to writing, I learned how to manage a team and the writing process.

After college, I worked at Acme as a social media manager, writing copy and social content for the company blog. However, I raised my hand to work on the communications plan for a product launch, where I discovered my interest in product marketing.

After switching to a product marketing role and managing the two most successful new product launches last year, I realized I was excited to take on a new position. I've learned I work best on products that I love and use, and given that I'm a big user of your company's products, I jumped at the chance to apply when I saw the open posting.

Sample 6

Hi! My name is John D'souza, and I am 30 years old. I have over seven years of experience as an Operations lead at Crompton Greaves.

I have a data analysis background, studying Information Systems at Calcutta University. Throughout my career, I have accomplished some impressive feats. For instance, at Crompton Greaves, I spearheaded a project to migrate all operational data to a new data warehousing system to reduce costs. The new solution was a much better fit for our business, ultimately leading to savings of up to Rs. 10,00,000 annually.

Sample 7

I have worked in the customer service industry for 12 years, and currently, I work as a customer service representative in the tech sector, where I handle incoming calls. This job is rewarding because it allows me to interact with people and assist them with their concerns.

In addition, I enjoy tackling the challenges that come with the role. Recently, I implemented a creative approach to enhance client relations, resulting in a 40% increase in sales within six months.

Sample 8

I am passionate about digital marketing and consciously try to learn something new daily. In my previous job, I honed my digital marketing skills. However, I had to leave the role due to unforeseen circumstances.

While I enjoyed my previous job, I am now seeking a company that offers long-term career growth opportunities. This position aligns well with my skills and interests, and I am confident I can contribute meaningfully to the team.

Sample 9

I am an energetic healthcare professional with five years of experience in the field. My passion for healthcare drives me to constantly seek new ways to enhance my medical, technical, and interpersonal skills.

I have been a personal nurse for three years, providing compassionate patient care. This experience has allowed me to develop essential skills such as empathy, strong interpersonal skills, and technical proficiency.

In addition, I have honed my communication and time management skills over the last four years, working closely with individuals in various settings. I am grateful for the skills I have acquired through my current job.

I am excited about the opportunity to work as a resident nurse in a hospital setting. This job opening is an ideal fit for my skills and career aspirations, and I am eager to contribute my expertise to the team.

Sample 10

Currently, I am an account executive at Husain And Company, responsible for managing top clients. I find this job fulfilling as I am passionate about numbers and accounting practices and enjoy the challenges that come with it.

While I appreciate my current role's opportunities, I seek to work in an organization offering clear career growth opportunities. I am excited about this position as it aligns well with my skills and interests and provides the potential for long-term career development.

"The hard days are what make you stronger."

A 2 Tell Me Something About Yourself That's Not On Your Resume

An interviewer might phrase the question, Tell us something about yourself that is not on your resume in different ways, such as What should I know that's not on your resume? Your goal is to share something interesting about yourself that illuminates why you are the best fit for the job. Their goal is to get to know your on-the-job attitude and experience.

Be honest, brief, and confident. Please have a few things ready to share and tie them to your mindset and skills, which are valuable in the job. Share a strength that isn't on your resume.

Before you begin speaking, take a second to gather your thoughts. Keep your response clear and organized. Storytelling can be a valuable interview tool, but get to the point and be concise to respect the interviewer's time. You don't need to appear nervous to answer this question effectively.

Interviewers ask this question to understand your personality and character beyond your work experiences and accomplishments. You can choose from three primary themes for your response. First, discuss one of your positive traits, such as creativity, enthusiasm, tenacity, or dedication. Second, share a story or detail that reveals something extraordinary about you and your accomplishments. Lastly, talk about your motivation or overall goal.

Avoid mentioning anything written on your resume or cover letter. Also, avoid overly personal information or anything that raises a red flag. Instead, bring up your work ethic or something that connects your answer to the position.

Begin by explaining your trait or story. Then, summarize why it's essential for the interviewer to know this. Connect your answer to the job, the company, or both. Here's a template for your response: I'd like you to know [strength/anecdote]. This is important because [explanation of what it shows about you]. This will help me with [aspect of the job] because (something that connects your answer to the position.)

Sample 1

I want to highlight my strong organizational skills and successful event planning track record. Throughout my experiences, I've developed a habit of staying well-organized and efficient in my work. My managers have consistently recognized me as a key facilitator in keeping teams on track.

Recently, I had the opportunity to plan a conference for our customers to educate them on our new product line. I was responsible for organizing every aspect of the event and was thrilled to receive such positive feedback from attendees.

Overall, my determination and attention to detail are qualities that I bring to every job I do. I strive for perfection in everything I undertake, and I believe this mindset will make me an invaluable asset to any team.

Sample 2

I attribute my sales record to my competitive nature. I'm always looking for new challenges. In my free time, you can usually find me training. I also value the peace and focus I've gained through continuous improvement efforts.

I visit yard sales to find interesting items. I have built a good collection, learned to value things, and improved my negotiation skills!

Sample 3

I chose not to include my coding skills on my resume because this job seems more focused on graphic design and branding. However, I have experience with HTML, CSS, and JavaScript, and I am interested in using these skills on various web development projects I could be assigned to.

Sample 4

I have an intense curiosity about the world around me, which I communicate to my students, and I cultivate excitement about learning new things, especially in science.

For example, I developed a unit about the weather and shared my fascination with different types of clouds and the relationship between cloud types and weather patterns.

This inspired several of my students to meet for a weather club after class.

Sample 5

One thing distinguishing me from many other salespeople is my ability to connect with clients on a human level right from the beginning. I focus on making them feel comfortable and uncovering all their pressing needs related to my product. By doing this, I can conversationally present my product, tailored specifically to their needs. My skill in small talk is a key factor in my success, as it allows me to warm-up customers and build rapport. In addition, I am genuinely interested in sports and current events, which help me, connect with a wide range of clients and engage in meaningful conversations with them.

Sample 6

My ability to build solid relationships and connect with others is a significant strength of mine. While my resume showcases my professional achievements, my interpersonal skills have enabled me to accomplish those things. I value building positive relationships with all stakeholders, including clients, coworkers, direct reports, and managers. I believe that this genuine care and concern for others is something that people can feel, and it helps me to establish trust and credibility with them.

For example, when we were at risk of losing a key client last year, I took the initiative to investigate the issue and find a solution. By collaborating with our sales and development teams, I identified the root cause of the problem and proposed a solution that met everyone's needs. As a result of this effort, we could retain the client and even increase their business by 18%.

Sample 7

As the organizer of a runners' group that meets every weekend for a distance run, I have gained valuable experience in social media outreach and event coordination. When I first moved to the area, I posted a flyer at the local gym to start the group. However, I quickly realized that social media would be a more effective way to reach a larger audience. I leveraged my skills in social media communication to promote the group and manage its event calendar. Over time, the group has grown from just a few individuals to a diverse community of 30 runners committed to improving their health and fitness. Through my entrepreneurial spirit and passion for empowering others, I have built a strong sense of camaraderie and motivation within the group. I believe these skills and experiences would be highly applicable to a role as a social media coordinator.

Sample 8

I am a multifaceted individual with a diverse range of interests. I am an abstract artist with a keen eye for creativity and design. Despite my artistic passions, I am a civil engineer, which has given me a deep appreciation for structure and problem-solving.

I love to read in my free time and am passionate about exploring new books. I have a great sense of style and enjoy following fashion trends closely. Additionally, I strongly prefer cleanliness and take pride in maintaining a neat and organized living and workspace.

While I prefer to spend my weekends indoors with a good book, I also have a soft spot for my two dogs, Casey and Betsy, who have become a cherished part of my family. If I venture out, I prefer solo trips and have recently enjoyed exploring Shimla. Finally, I also love gardening, particularly when it comes to fresh flowers.

Sample 9

Hi, I am Frank. I am from Kolkata. I completed my Micro Biology Honours from St. Xaviers' College. My family includes my father, an educationalist; my mother, a teacher; and my brother, who works as head of HR at a firm in Mumbai.

I love swimming and have represented my school in district and state-level competitions. I am also a part of the Rotary Club, where I have participated in community service at various schools, teaching the underprivileged and visiting several old age homes.

Being part of the Rotary Club has given me a different perspective on life, making me appreciate what I am and where I am.

Sample 10

I have worked in the education industry for the past four years. My most recent role was as a Branch Manager at a Play School, where I coordinated and managed the school's day-to-day operations. My leadership abilities and strong communication skills fostered a healthy atmosphere driven by team spirit amongst the teachers and staff. As a mentor, I taught the teachers life skills, which they passed on to the school's children. I am seeking an opportunity to work in a company that values teamwork and group dynamics, where I can leverage my experience and learning to contribute towards the organization's growth.

"I hated every minute of training, but I said, Don't quit. Suffer now and live the rest of your life as a champion."

B 1 Strengths Samples

1. Dedicated

Dedication could mean being committed to your work, putting in extra effort to achieve your goals, or being persistent while facing challenges.

I worked in a team on a time-sensitive project in my previous job. I put in extra hours and worked weekends to ensure we met our deadlines and delivered high-quality results.

In my personal life, I am dedicated to staying fit and healthy. I make time for regular exercise and healthy eating, even when it's challenging or inconvenient.

Another way I demonstrate dedication is by taking the time to learn and develop new skills. I always seek opportunities to grow and improve through workshops, training programs, or self-study.

2. Creative

The strength that I am most proud of is my creativity. I enjoy pushing the boundaries and thinking outside the box to accomplish things few, if any, have done. Thanks to this mindset, I have won several graphic design competitions for my work.

Essentially, this means you are a resourceful, intelligent, and innovative individual.

3. Flexible

I consider myself a highly flexible individual who can quickly adapt to changes. Whether transitioning from one client to another or switching from one project to the next, I can maintain my focus and diligently complete my tasks without hindering my workflow or progress. Given the diverse clientele that your agency serves, I am confident that my flexibility could be a valuable asset to your team.

This means you are versatile, adaptable, and easily handle various tasks and situations.

4. Resourceful

I believe that one of my greatest strengths is my resourcefulness. Whenever a problem arises, I can develop innovative solutions and am committed to finding a resolution. I never give up until I find a way to overcome the challenge.

In essence, this means that you are a problem-solver determined to find solutions to any obstacles that come your way.

5. Problem-solving skills

I consider my problem-solving skills to be my greatest strength. When faced with a crisis or challenging situation, I feel compelled to find a solution quickly and accurately. My approach involves analyzing the problem, evaluating various options to determine the best course of action, and then discussing the plan with my team before implementing it. I am confident that my strong analytical abilities would make me a valuable asset to your team.

In essence, this means that you are a skilled problem-solver who is also highly analytical in finding solutions.

6. Ability to work under pressure

I possess the ability to work effectively and efficiently under pressure. When faced with a crisis, I understand the importance of remaining calm and composed, as panicking can only worsen the situation and impede progress. I am confident in adapting to challenging circumstances and working diligently to achieve positive outcomes.

In essence, this means that you are adaptable and flexible in your approach to work, able to remain calm under pressure and achieve positive results even in challenging situations.

7. Time management skills

I would say that my greatest strength is my proficiency in time management. As someone who places a high value on punctuality, I always strive to meet my deadlines and complete my tasks on time. I find it helpful to establish specific time frames for each task to stay on track and manage my time effectively.

In essence, this means that you are a punctual and diligent individual who values the importance of time management and is skilled at organizing and prioritizing tasks to meet deadlines.

8. Team player

I am a team player and have always preferred working collaboratively. I firmly believe that effective teamwork is built on communication, trust, and motivation among team members. To promote a positive team dynamic, I actively encourage and inspire my colleagues, always striving to foster a supportive and collaborative working environment.

In essence, this means that you are a motivated and passionate individual who understands the importance of teamwork and is committed to promoting a positive and supportive team environment.

9. Fast learner

I would say that my greatest strength is my ability to learn quickly. Fortunately, I have a natural aptitude for learning new concepts and skills. In my previous role, I completed a training program in one-third of the time it took others. I am also a resourceful learner, and I often turn to online tutorials, such as YouTube videos, to learn new software and tools.

In essence, this means that you are a knowledgeable and adaptable individual with a natural aptitude for learning quickly and who is resourceful in seeking new information and skills.

10. Leadership skills

Leading and motivating my team to achieve their best results is one of my greatest strengths. I have always had strong leadership skills, and even during my school days, I served as a class representative and house leader. In my previous role, I was promoted to a team leader position after just one year, and our team received recognition from other departments for our exceptional teamwork and productivity.

In essence, this means that you are an inspirational and effective leader capable of motivating and guiding teams toward achieving their best results.

11. Respectfulness

Respectfulness could mean showing consideration for others, treating everyone with dignity and kindness, or being open-minded and accepting of different perspectives.

I worked with colleagues from diverse backgrounds and different skill sets in my previous job. I made sure to treat everyone with equal respect and consideration, regardless of their position or level of expertise.

In my personal life, I believe in treating everyone with kindness and compassion. I try to listen to others and understand their perspectives, even if I don't always agree with them.

Another way I demonstrate respectfulness is by being mindful of other people's time and schedules. I always try to be punctual and ensure that I am not taking up too much of someone else's time.

By providing specific examples of how you exhibit respectfulness, you can show the interviewer that you're a team player, empathetic, and able to work well with others. These are all valuable qualities that make you a strong candidate for the position.

12. Writing skills

I consider my most vital asset to be my excellent writing skills. I carefully conduct thorough research to ensure my information is accurate and reliable. Moreover, I adapt my writing style to suit the target audience and their requirements. I have won several online writing competitions thanks to my creative writing abilities.

This means you are a skilled writer with a strong research orientation who can craft content tailored to a specific audience.

13. Determination

My greatest strength is my unwavering determination, which has enabled me to overcome various challenges and achieve my goals. I firmly believe in never giving up, whether it's in my personal or professional life. I always strive to work hard and deliver my best to complete my tasks on time.

This means you are a persistent and hard-working individual driven toward success.

14. Negotiation skills

Negotiation skills are my greatest strength in my professional (and sometimes personal) life. I have enhanced this skill through my five years as a salesperson, which is why I was promoted to sales manager in my previous organization in a short span. Thanks to it, I can build strong relationships with customers and clients.

In other words, this also means that you have strong interpersonal and communication skills.

15. Communication skills

My communication skills have helped me build strong relationships with colleagues and clients. To work efficiently, I believe that communication is the key. I listen actively and try to empathize with the people I speak with. This allows them to put their trust in me, which, I think, is not very easy to do in the business world.

In other words, you are an empathetic person with good listening skills.

16. Discipline

First, define what you mean by discipline. It could mean being organized, focused, sticking to a plan, or having the self-control to resist temptations or distractions.

In my previous job, I was responsible for meeting tight deadlines regularly. To ensure that I completed my work on time, I created a detailed schedule and stuck to it, even if it meant working late or putting in extra effort.

In my personal life, I am committed to maintaining a healthy lifestyle. This means sticking to a consistent exercise routine and making healthy food choices, even when indulging in unhealthy foods or skipping a workout is tempting.

17. Patience

First, define what you mean by patience. It could mean having the ability to stay calm and composed under pressure, or it could mean being able to wait for the right moment or outcome.

In my previous job, I worked with clients who often had a lot of questions or concerns. I found that by actively listening to their needs and taking the time to address their concerns, I was able to build stronger relationships and provide better service.

In my personal life, I enjoy cooking and trying out new recipes. Sometimes, things don't turn out as planned, but I've learned to stay patient and keep trying until I get it right. This has helped me become a better cook and taught me the value of persistence.

Another way I demonstrate patience is by taking the time to analyze complex problems or situations. Rather than rushing to a solution, I prefer carefully considering all the options and potential outcomes before deciding.

By providing specific examples of how you exhibit patience, you can show the interviewer that you're level-headed, attentive, and able to handle challenging situations gracefully. These are all valuable qualities that make you a strong candidate for the position.

18. Enthusiasm

Enthusiasm means having a positive attitude, being passionate about your work, or having a genuine interest in the job or industry.

In my previous job, I was part of a team working on a challenging project. I maintained a positive attitude and encouraged my colleagues to keep pushing forward, even when things got tough. My enthusiasm helped to keep everyone motivated and focused on the end goal.

In my personal life, I am passionate about volunteer work. I regularly volunteer at a local animal shelter, and I love making a difference in the lives of the animals and the community. My enthusiasm for this work has inspired others to participate and make a difference.

I demonstrate enthusiasm by staying up-to-date on industry news and trends. I enjoy reading articles, attending conferences, and networking with other professionals in my field. This helps me stay excited about my work and keeps me motivated to learn and grow.

By providing specific examples of how you exhibit enthusiasm, you can show the interviewer that you're driven, optimistic, and genuinely interested in the job and industry. These are all valuable qualities that make you a strong candidate for the position.

19. Trustworthiness

Trustworthiness could mean being honest, reliable, and keeping your commitments or being confidential and keeping sensitive information secure.

In my previous job, I was responsible for handling confidential client information. I took this responsibility seriously and ensured all the information was confidential. I also made sure to follow all the required protocols and procedures.

In my personal life, I believe in being honest and reliable in all my relationships. I am upfront and transparent with my friends and family and keep my promises and commitments.

Another way I demonstrate trustworthiness is by admitting my mistakes and taking responsibility for my actions. I believe that owning up to your mistakes is an integral part of being trustworthy and earning the trust of others.

By providing specific examples of your trustworthiness, you can show the interviewer that you're responsible, dependable, and can handle sensitive information carefully. These are all valuable qualities that make you a strong candidate for the position.

"The same boiling water that softens the potato hardens the egg. It's what you're made of. Not the circumstances."

B2 What Are Your Strengths?

List your top strengths. Aim for at least ten, and be creative. Jot down everything that comes to mind. It's essential to take the time to identify your strengths and practice talking about them. That way, you'll be ready when you walk into that interview. Show relevant background on topics critical to the job, including college degrees, certifications, training seminars, mentoring, internships, etc. Show your programming abilities in a desired language, writing proposals, selling widgets, litigating cases, organizing events, translating from Mandarin, etc. Competencies such as problem-solving, influencing, team building, negotiation, managing up, etc. describe your experience with specific software or type of task, expertise in a particular industry, a track record of working with similar products or clients, etc. If you have trouble coming up with enough work-related strength, jot down positive personality qualities or personal strengths. You may find ways to relate these to job performance. Describe at least five strengths that you are comfortable discussing. You may not talk about all of these strengths in every interview. Avoid weak praise and lame strengths. Pick something impressive. Don't use pleasant to work with as your main selling point. Choose strengths that you possess. Don't pick strength just because it's in the job description. Showcase the best and most authentic professional version of yourself. Demonstrate a concise example ready to back each of your strengths and do it concisely.

Feeling uncomfortable when asked to discuss your strengths is understandable, as you don't want to come across as bragging. However, your response to this question is crucial, as it can help the interviewer determine if your strengths align with the company's needs.

To answer this question effectively, you must follow these steps; a) Assess your hard skills, b) Assess your transferable skills c) Assess your traits.

Sample 1

My strength is my problem-solving skills (Assess your hard skills).In my current position as a customer service manager, I feel that my communication skills are top-level because I relate with senior executives on the same basis that I connect with junior staff members. (Transferable skills)

I was patient enough to turn a toxic work environment into a positive one and created a motivating environment where everyone could work comfortably. (Personal trait)

Sample 2

One of my greatest strengths is my attention to detail. I have always been naturally detail-oriented in my work and enjoy it. I noticed in your job description that this position involves a lot of detail-oriented work, which is one of the reasons I applied.

In my previous job, I managed 8-10 client projects simultaneously, each with about 75 different tasks. My attention to detail enabled me to complete all of my projects on time, and I finished 45% of them ahead of schedule.

Sample 3

One of my greatest strengths is as a problem solver. I can see a situation from different perspectives and accomplish my work despite challenging obstacles. I also feel that my communication skills are top-notch. I feel just as comfortable presenting to senior executives as mediating a conflict between junior team members. I previously worked as a programmer, so I have that developer perspective, and I think they respect me for that.

The candidate talks about how their problem-solving skills work (seeing things from different perspectives) and her communication skills (presenting to senior leaders and mediating team disputes).

Sample 4

My greatest professional strength is handling pressure and working under tight deadlines. This skill helped me succeed in this position because of the many clients and deadlines.

In my last position, I handled complex projects on short notice for several top clients, like Coca-Cola and Microsoft. I completed 100% of the projects I was assigned, resulting in us winning 50 lakhs more in additional business from these clients.

Notice that the answer goes beyond hard work, which is too general. Anybody can say that they work hard. With a specific example, this candidate clarifies what work ethic means and talks about being deadline-driven and reliable.

Sample 5

I want to share that I possess exceptional writing skills gained through my five-year copyeditor experience. This has instilled in me a strong attention to detail in my writing. My experience writing for various publications has taught me how to tailor my writing style to suit the specific task and audience.

As a marketing assistant, I am confident in writing and editing press releases effectively and updating web content accurately and easily. I believe that my skills will be beneficial in this role, and I can make valuable contributions to the team.

Sample 6

I believe that this job is a perfect fit for my experience and interests. Firstly, I am highly organized and efficient in keeping a department running smoothly. I have experience with the challenges that arise in a busy marketing department, and I enjoy the details of scheduling, prioritizing, organizing, and following up.

On the other hand, I am also a creative individual, which I believe is a great asset in marketing, especially in an innovative company like this one. I enjoy creating creative solutions to problems, such as the fashion trivia contest I developed for ShopSpree.com, which significantly increased site sign-ups.

Moreover, I am a team player and enjoy collaborating with others, especially creative ones. I believe teamwork is crucial in achieving a common goal, and I am always willing to go above and beyond to help my team members.

Finally, I am known for my reliability and ability to perform under pressure. For instance, I recall rushing to the printer at 1 am to pick up and collate presentations for a big 8 am meeting. I am confident that my skills and experience would be an asset to your team, and I am excited about the opportunity to contribute to your company's success.

Sample 7

My background as an English major has provided me with the necessary skills to excel in this position. In my previous job, I was responsible for restructuring, editing, and writing the employee newsletter for the hospital. By featuring employee profiles and contributions, I created a new format that was more widely read and appreciated by staff, which helped boost morale. Additionally, I was able to simplify the language used in significant sections of the employee handbook, making it more accessible and user-friendly for all staff members.

Sample 8

My biggest strength is my ability to pick up new skills quickly. As you may have seen on my resume, I've worked various odd jobs, such as housekeeping, cooking, and more. In most of these positions, I acquired all the necessary skills within 1 or 2 weeks, even with little or no prior experience. Although I don't have any experience as a bartender, I have the required certification, and I'm confident that I can become proficient at the job within a few weeks.

Sample 9

I have a strong work ethic and excellent writing skills. When working on a project, I don't just aim to meet the deadlines; I strive to complete my work well ahead of schedule. I also have a keen attention to detail, especially in my writing. I've gained extensive experience in content writing over the past three years, working for various publications that required me to meet strict deadlines while ensuring the quality of my work.

Sample 10

One of my strengths is my ability to communicate and collaborate with others effectively. I find it easy to build rapport with colleagues, clients, and stakeholders, which helps me work effectively with people from diverse backgrounds and different levels of expertise. I believe that effective communication is essential to achieving our goals as a team, and I am always willing to lend an ear and offer support when needed.

As a project manager, I led a team of designers, developers, and copywriters to launch a new e-commerce website for a client. During the project, I regularly checked in with team members to ensure they were on track, and I provided feedback and guidance to help them overcome any challenges they faced. By fostering open communication and collaboration, we completed the project on time and within budget while exceeding the client's expectations.

"Work like someone is working twenty-four hours a day to take it away from you."

C1 Weakness Samples

1. Procrastination

I have been working on overcoming procrastination. In the past, I would put off tasks until the last minute, causing unnecessary stress. I have realized the importance of prioritizing tasks and planning to avoid last-minute pressure. I have improved my productivity and time management skills by actively working on these strategies.

2. Impatient

I tend to be impatient when working with time, sometimes leading to rushing through tasks or projects. In the past, I often sought out job profiles where I could work independently to accommodate this tendency. However, as my career has progressed, I have come to appreciate the value of teamwork and collaboration. I have actively developed my patience and team-building skills by attending workshops and seeking colleague feedback. This has helped me become a better team player and contributor in the workplace.

3. Insecurity

As an introvert, I sometimes struggle with self-confidence, leading to insecurity about my work. Even after conducting thorough research and paying close attention to details, I may doubt my work and second-guess myself. However, I am actively working to overcome this by seeking constructive feedback and building my skills through ongoing learning and development opportunities.

4. Self-criticism

I can be pretty self-critical, so I tend to be hard on myself. Even when others tell me my work is good, I wonder if I could have done better. In the past, this has led me to overwork and obsess over every little detail, even after receiving praise and appreciation. However, I am working on this by trying to look at my achievements objectively, and this has made a significant difference in my professional life.

5. Disorganized

My biggest weakness is that I struggle with being organized. Although it has not affected my work thus far, I recognize that my workspace can become quite messy. To address this, I am actively working on improving my organizational skills. I have started developing a habit of tidying and organizing my desk and inbox at the end of each working day. I have already noticed significant progress in this area.

6. Blunt

Sometimes I can come across as too blunt when giving feedback to my team. While honesty is important, I have learned that not everyone responds well to direct feedback. To improve in this area, I have been taking an online leadership management course and focusing on developing better communication skills. I am also taking the time to get to know my team better and understand their communication styles so that I can deliver feedback in a way that is more effective and tailored to their needs.

7. Public speaking

Public speaking is one of my biggest weaknesses, so I took a public speaking course. Although my job profile doesn't require public speaking skills, it is still an area I knew I needed to improve. I can honestly say that the course helped me because I can now stand up in meetings and express my thoughts with more confidence and clarity.

8. Shy by nature

My weakness is that I tend to be shy by nature. While I have great ideas and insights to contribute during team meetings, my shyness sometimes holds me back from speaking up. However, I recognized that this hindered my professional growth and decided to act. I have been working on my confidence and communication skills by attending public speaking workshops and joining social clubs to meet new people. These efforts have helped me become more comfortable in group settings and better express my ideas.

9. Too detail-oriented

I can be too detail-oriented sometimes, focusing on one specific detail for a long time and ignoring the big picture. This was a very stressful way of working, as I often faced problems when the deadline was approaching. However, in the past year, I realized I needed to improve. I have learned to prioritize each project and not spend too much time on one minor detail. This has helped me work more efficiently and productively.

10. Saying No.

One of my weaknesses is having difficulty saying 'No' when my colleagues or supervisors make requests. I tend to take on more than I can handle, leading to burnout. To address this, I have started using a project management app and only agree to requests if I have time outside my current workload. This has helped me manage my time better and avoid over-committing myself.

11. Unhealthy work/life balance

I have struggled to maintain a healthy work-life balance as a success-driven person. I tended to overwork to the point where I was not giving enough attention to my personal life. After realizing how my work impacted my relationships with loved ones, I knew I needed to change. I started by setting specific boundaries for my personal and professional life, such as dedicating time after work hours solely to spending time with my family or myself without checking work emails or messages. This has helped me tremendously, and I now feel happier and more fulfilled at work and in my personal life.

12. Delegating

Because I am self-motivated and self-sufficient, I often struggle with delegating responsibility to my team, wanting to complete the task alone. After getting promoted to a managerial position, it became clear that I had to delegate responsibilities as I couldn't handle everything alone. So, gradually, I learned to trust my team and started implementing a project management system. This system helps me oversee the project's progress and has allowed us to work more efficiently as a team.

13. Multitasking

While multitasking can be beneficial, it is also a weakness for me. I tend to work on multiple projects simultaneously, which can cause me to lose focus and not perform at my best. To overcome this, I have started prioritizing my tasks and focusing on one project at a time. I have also started using project management tools to help me stay organized and on track, which has helped me increase my productivity and meet my deadlines more efficiently.

14. Hard skills

Articulate Storyline is one software I still need to familiarise myself with. Although it is not necessary now, I think it will be a helpful tool that will work to our advantage in the future. I have been teaching myself the basics via Youtube tutorials and, at the same time, looking for online courses.

15. Micromanaging

I am a person who values goals and meeting deadlines. When promoted to team leader, I wanted to ensure that our projects were delivered on time and without errors. To achieve this, I began micromanaging my team. However, over time, I realized that although we met our deadlines, micromanaging stifled creativity and limited my team's self-worth. So, I decided to trust my team's abilities and implement a project management system to oversee the project's progress. This change proved to be helpful for both my team and myself.

"The miracle is not that we do this work, but that we are happy to do it."

C2 What Are Your Weaknesses?

Recruiters ask this question because they are more concerned about how you answer it. You shouldn't lie. It would help if you were careful not to give formula answers that are not close to being your weakness. Answers like My greatest weakness is that I am so much of a perfectionist; I love everything to be organized and orderly all the time. This is a perfect answer, but this is a common line that sounds unrealistic and doesn't reflect an actual weakness.

First, you must be self-aware to recognize your real weakness. Be careful when choosing a weakness so that it does not affect your getting the job. It would help if you were sure you were talking about a real weakness (Truthful). After telling the recruiter about your weakness, you should also state the effort that you are putting in to manage the weakness that you stated (Self-improvement).

Ultimately, you want to discuss your weaknesses in a way that helps you gain ground rather than lose it. Keep in mind that what hiring managers want to know is how you handle adversity. Make a list of your known shortcomings, and one way to gather material is from past performance evaluations and notes from supervisors about areas for improvement. Make sure to research the employer and the open position. Thoroughly review the job posting so you don't identify something as a deficiency that's essential to the job. Re-read the job description so you know what attributes and abilities are critical to the performance of the job. Those hard or soft skills shouldn't be on your weakness list. Everything else is fair game.

Sample 1

I have primarily focused on the design aspect of projects in my previous experiences, which has limited my exposure to content development. However, I recognize the importance of well-written content and am eager to expand my skills. I am confident that I can quickly learn and improve my writing abilities to meet the needs of any future job requirements.

Sample 2

While I believe it's important to have a critical eye toward one's work, I have noticed that I tend to focus too much on my weaknesses rather than my strengths. I understand that acknowledging and celebrating one's accomplishments is just as important as identifying areas for improvement. To address this, I have been making a conscious effort to cultivate a positive self-image. This includes practicing three positive thoughts for every negative and reciting self-affirmations daily. This will help me better appreciate my strengths and contribute to a healthier work-life balance.

Sample 3

While I enjoy working independently, teamwork is often necessary to accomplish larger goals. I have struggled with patience when working in a team, as I prefer working at my own pace. However, I am actively working to improve in this area by seeking team-building opportunities and learning to trust my colleagues better. I believe effective collaboration is essential for success in any endeavor, and I am committed to becoming a more patient and effective team player.

Sample 4

One area where I am constantly working to improve is my organizational skills. I get so absorbed in my work that I sometimes overlook the importance of keeping things in order. However, I recognize that staying organized is crucial for maintaining a professional image, and I have addressed this weakness. I have started using reminder apps to set aside time each day to tidy up my workspace and home environment, and I have already seen improvement in my ability to keep things in order. While it is still a work in progress, I am committed to becoming a more organized and efficient worker.

Sample 5

I must admit that public speaking has always made me a bit nervous, despite my role as a graphic designer not requiring it very often. However, I recognize the importance of effective communication in any workplace, and I believe public speaking is a valuable skill to develop. To confront this fear, I spoke with my manager and expressed my desire to take on more speaking opportunities, such as giving introductory speeches during team meetings. Through this experience, I have become more comfortable speaking in front of others and have improved my communication ability with my colleagues. While I still have some work to do in this area, I am committed to continued growth and development as a communicator.

Sample 6

Procrastination was a significant challenge, and my friends often teased me. However, I have overcome this weakness by adopting a more proactive approach to my work. When assigned a new project, I begin thinking about it and mentally composing my first and second drafts. With a strong command of grammar, I can quickly finalize my work without spending much time proofreading or revising. When I started working as a content writer, I realized that this process was effective for me, and I have never missed a deadline since. To ensure that I stay on track, I set early deadlines at least 24 hours before the deadline, allowing me to complete my work well in advance and with time to spare.

Sample 7

My weakness is my tendency to take on more than I can handle, both physically and mentally. At my previous job, I was constantly busy and struggling to catch up, which was stressful and overwhelming. To address this habit, I prioritize tasks to allocate my time and energy more effectively. This approach helps me feel calmer and more clear-headed as I work on my projects, and I find that I produce better results when I have enough time to complete my work. Additionally, I am trying to enjoy my time outside of work to ensure that I return to the office feeling recharged and ready to take on new challenges rather than burnt out.

Sample 8

The area I improved on in the past is my salesmanship skills. As a product manager who works with internal teams and does not interface with clients or sales prospects, I don't do any selling in my role. However, since I frequently communicate with the sales team, I felt it might benefit me to understand their strategies and tactics better. I took a sales skills course online. It improved how I work with sales teams, and now, when I join sales meetings, I have a better idea of what's going on, and I feel more effective in communicating with the sales team. This course also helped me build upon the skills I use to sell my vision for the product internally.

Sample 9

My greatest strength is my attention to detail. However, I have sometimes found myself getting too caught up in perfectionism. This has led me to spend excessive time triple-checking spreadsheets or tweaking presentation layouts. To address this, I have learned to manage my time more effectively and assess which tasks require this level of precision. I focus my energy on those tasks while still delivering high-quality work for other tasks that require attention to detail.

Sample 10

I am naturally introverted, sometimes making connecting with new people difficult and becoming comfortable in group settings. However, I recognize the importance of building strong relationships and working collaboratively with others. I have been developing my interpersonal skills to overcome my shyness, such as active listening, asking questions, and engaging in small talk. I also attend networking events and social gatherings to meet new people and expand my comfort zone. While it is still a work in progress, I am proud and will continue to push myself out of my comfort zone to build strong relationships in my personal and professional life.

"I am convinced that life is 10% what happens to me and 90% of how I react to it."

D 1 What Are Your Strengths And Weaknesses?

Focus primarily on your strengths during the interview. Show the interviewer how you actively overcome your weaknesses by discussing improvement steps. It's essential, to be honest about your real weakness but mention how you plan to fix it.

Ensure that your strengths and weaknesses do not contradict each other. To prepare for the interview, research the position you are applying for and identify areas where you can use your strengths.

Choose a weakness that is acceptable for the job at hand. Avoid confusing interests with strengths or dislikes with weaknesses.

Sample 1

I would describe myself as self-confident, honest, and enthusiastic, with a strong commitment to completing tasks on time. While I appreciate working with like-minded individuals, I enjoy engaging with people from diverse backgrounds and treating them respectfully.

That being said, I can become frustrated if a project or task is not completed on time. Additionally, while I value my intuition, I recognize the importance of making decisions with a clear mind.

Sample 2

My strength is my flexibility in handling change. As a customer service manager at my last job, I successfully turned around a hostile working environment and developed a highly supportive team.

As for my weakness, I tend to feel a sense of urgency to complete tasks, and I prioritize meeting deadlines. However, I have struggled with being organized in the past. To address this, I have implemented a time management system that has greatly improved my organizational skills.

Sample 3

Regarding my strengths, I would say that I can work well under pressure and meet tight deadlines, both proactively and reactively. Additionally, I possess excellent verbal and written communication skills, intercultural competency, and the ability to handle difficult personalities easily.

However, I am weak when hearing about sadness or difficult situations others face. I think about it too much and sometimes lose control of my emotions.

Sample 4

My strength lies in my extensive knowledge, which gives me the confidence to tackle complex challenges. I am a positive thinker and am skilled at building relationships with others. Additionally, I have a strong understanding of human psychology and am dedicated to achieving results efficiently while maintaining a pleasant demeanor.

Although I can generally control my anger, I am improving it. I can become frustrated when things are not completed on time. Still, I always strive to maintain a professional attitude and quickly return to my normal state once the issue is resolved.

Sample 5

I am a determined and dedicated individual who puts forth my total effort into any task I undertake. When I decide to take on a project, I commit all my strength and focus to achieving my goals.

I am a big-picture thinker, but I can sometimes miss small details. To address this, I make sure to have someone on my team who is detail-oriented to help me with this aspect. I can also be assertive in pursuing my goals.

Sample 6

My strength lies in my ability to turn hostile work environments into positive ones by developing a supportive team. I can also manage multiple projects and ensure deadlines are met.

However, one weakness I have noticed is that I sometimes become impatient, particularly when I want to finish things quickly. To address this, I am currently working on re-evaluating my to-do list and prioritizing tasks more effectively.

Sample 7

I am very comfortable working with different groups of people. My strength is my analytical and planning skills, which have developed over the years. It helps me to complete my work before the deadline.

As far as weaknesses, I feel that my management skills could be more robust, and I am constantly working to improve them. I am also slightly nervous while speaking in a group, but I have given many presentations to overcome this.

Sample 8

I am proficient in several programming languages, including HTML, C++, Java, and AppleScript. I have a track record of generating over 100% excess revenue for two separate companies by optimizing programming efficiency. Additionally, I have leadership experience with a team of five IT professionals in developing popular iPhone apps.

However, I do recognize that I tend to remain quiet in meetings. I am actively working on speaking up when I have ideas to share and contributing more to group discussions.

Sample 9

I am a highly motivated individual committed to seeing tasks through to completion. I understand the importance of my colleagues' time and the company's resources and strive to be an asset rather than a liability.

However, I have been told that sometimes I can be too much of a perfectionist. I have attended seminars focused on developing better self-management skills to address this.

Sample 10

I have several strengths; namely, I am patient, committed, honest, and self-motivated. I am also a big dreamer and forgive easily without holding grudges in my heart.

However, my greatest weakness is that I do not appreciate interruptions when I am focused on a task. Additionally, I tend to trust people easily, which can sometimes lead to disappointment. As a patient person, I am actively working on improving this flaw.

"Hard work beats talent when talent doesn't work hard."

D 2 What Are Your Pet Peeves? (Annoyance)

The attitude you express in your response will be evaluated based on your personality. It can be challenging because it requires you to talk about things that annoy you, which could make you sound negative or disagreeable. You may come across as unpleasant to work with, so it is essential to consider how you respond. Some people prefer to answer by saying they have no pet peeves. However, a better answer will focus on something that does not bother you much, that you can control, and that does not reflect poorly on you as an employee.

A) One way to answer this question is to focus on a pet peeve unrelated to the job. For example, your pet peeve might be people who do not use their blinkers when they drive. This type of answer will prevent you from saying something negative that is related to the job.

B) You can also describe a pet peeve related to the workplace. For instance, if the job involves a lot of teamwork, you might say that your pet peeve is when a person cannot work effectively with a group. However, be sure to explain how you would deal with that situation.

C) You might also turn this question around and emphasize your work standards. For example, you could say that you dislike when people do not challenge themselves to surpass the bare minimum, so you constantly push yourself to achieve the best results on any project.

Sample 1

I don't particularly appreciate when people have negative attitudes, particularly in the workplace. I like to remain positive, even during difficult situations, and I do not let people's negative attitudes affect me. Therefore, I proactively handle annoying situations.

Sample 2

If you were to ask my teenage daughter, she would probably tell you that my pet peeve is the volume of her music and the mess in her room. However, I do not have any other specific pet peeves. Whenever something bothers me, I take a step back, analyze the situation, and find a good solution to the problem. Therefore, I handle annoying situations proactively.

Sample 3

I'm not too fond of it when a team member refuses to carry their weight on a project. As team members, it is our job to help the entire team succeed. When I see someone not completing their task, I communicate my concerns clearly and effectively with the team. I try to come up with a solution, such as redistributing some of the tasks.

Sample 4

One of my pet peeves is when people are regularly late. My son constantly runs late for school, so I have struggled to inspire his timeliness. Timeliness is also vital in the workplace, whether it's simply showing up to work on time or meeting a deadline for an assignment. I am always punctual.

Sample 5

Something that bothers me at work is when my colleagues yell across the office to communicate with each other. This can be very distracting, making it difficult to focus on achieving my goals while working. When possible, I try to use noise-canceling headphones and listen to calming music to remain focused and not get distracted by my colleagues' conversations.

Sample 6

It can be annoying when my peers have negative attitudes. I like to maintain a positive mindset and am optimistic about my work. Hearing fellow staff members speak negatively about their work or the workplace can be discouraging. To manage this, I sometimes counter their negative claims with positive ones to shift the conversation towards more uplifting topics.

Sample 7

I noticed that one of my co-workers always seemed to interrupt me when I was in the middle of making a point. For a few weeks, I felt frustrated. However, I decided to speak to him one-on-one about what was happening. After our conversation, the interruptions stopped. He hadn't realized how his behavior was affecting me.

Sample 8

I am an introvert, and sometimes I have struggled to adjust to noisy open offices where it is normal for people to play loud music or hold long conversations. But I have figured out how to find quiet space when I need to concentrate. I wear headphones or book an empty office or conference room.

Sample 9

I have worked where some people leading meetings did not seem to use the time as efficiently as they could have, making me feel unproductive. To address this issue, I have tried to provide a model for how things could be different. I do this by running my meetings in a streamlined way and distributing agendas beforehand.

Sample 10

One of my pet peeves is when I work on group projects, and some team members don't contribute as much as they can. I enjoy collaborating with colleagues and believe teams are great for executing successful projects. However, I find it frustrating when others don't try to work together and meaningfully contribute to the team's success. To address this, I maintain constant communication with my teams and establish clear expectations.

"In the middle of every difficulty lies opportunity."

E 1 What Do You Know About Our Company?

The goal is to determine if a candidate has invested little time on the company's website and looked through online materials. It would help determine who the leading players are and understand the company. Research, well, a rule of thumb here is to do some Googling and learn the following about the company:

- What does their product or service do?
- What impact do the products/services have?
- What's the company culture like?
- What is the latest news about the company? How are they performing?
- Whatever other type of info you can dig up

The company and position that appeal to you and which requirements fit your skills and experience. Your answer should emphasize what you can contribute to the company and what you will bring to the position. Mention any skills or work experience that makes you a unique and strong candidate.

Most importantly, you want to communicate your enthusiasm about the company and its industry to your potential employer. During your interview, ensuring the hiring manager understands how much you want to work for the organization is a good idea. You can express this with a strong understanding of the company's business type. You can also get your enthusiasm across by discussing how your strengths match the company's goals. However, the key factor in demonstrating your enthusiasm is coming across as honest. Don't go overboard and make yourself seem artificially excited during the interview process, or your interviewer could immediately reconsider you for potential hiring.

Sample 1

I searched for information about your company on Google and found good reviews and interesting news. Additionally, your former employees have spoken highly of you on social media. As a result, I believe that I now have a good understanding of your working environment.

Sample 2

Volunteering has always been an important part of my life, which was set as an example by my parents. While researching potential employers, I was impressed by your company's long-standing dedication to community service. I found it exciting to learn that your personnel can use up to 7 days of paid time to volunteer. I was also pleased to hear about the charity golf tournament the company sponsors annually, which brings everyone together. Working for an organization that actively supports our community would be great.

Sample 3

I have read a lot about your company and find the open space offices, lounge for employees, and team-building activities you organize very interesting. It seems like a great place to work and grow professionally, at least based on the information I have found.

Sample 4

I understand that your company is one of the largest providers of payroll software and was founded in 2012 when your CEO realized that many small businesses were spending more than they should on payroll, which hindered their growth. The story on your website's about us page was fascinating, and there appears to be a significant demand for your product, given your rapid growth. Your company doubled in size last year and is on track to do it again this year.

Sample 5

I appreciate that the company was founded in 2006 by Angelina Smith. I feel a strong connection to the mission and values of this company, and I am very impressed by how much it has grown in recent years. The work that your team did for HUDCO was both innovative and heartfelt. I always wanted to be a part of the creative team here.

Sample 6

I know your company is one of the largest investment banks in India, with headquarters in Mumbai and a workforce of 25,000 employees, per your website. I have been working in the same industry for a few years and have known about your company for some time. Your company is one of the most prominent names in the industry, which is why I was excited to apply for the job when I saw it posted on your website.

Sample 7

I have researched quite a bit about your company and admire your mission of creating and providing highly engaging brain games for mobile audiences of all ages. Additionally, your engineering and design teams have built a world-class technology platform that allows millions to play at any time and from any device.

I appreciate that your company fosters and supports continuous innovation in your culture and encourages teams to try, test, fail, and then start again with projects and learn from their experiences. This approach resonates with me.

I also like that your company supports open office spaces and flexible work hours. Your big goal for 2025, moving into the international market, sounds challenging and exciting.

I believe that my technical skills and strong work ethic can align well with your company's culture,

Sample 8

I highly respect your company's commitment to constantly evolving. Growth and innovation are key in any industry, especially in technology, and your organization is consistently pushing past preconceived limitations. In the past year alone, you have taken several risks as you entered different markets, all of which have paid off.

As an engineer, I always strive to approach problems in new and creative ways. I am confident I can bring a fresh perspective and be an asset to this team.

Sample 9

Founded by three friends in 2006, your company has provided what most corporations couldn't offer: a reliable business model, work-life balance, and a commitment to giving back to society.

Since the early days of your firm, like many others, I knew that your company had the potential to become a major player in the industry. The ABC program you started for the XYZ community is still gaining attention, and I am impressed by how your company takes care of its employees through a proper work-life balance.

As a firm believer in teamwork, I am confident that your company will provide me with ample opportunities to showcase my abilities alongside a skilled workforce.

Sample 10

I appreciate that your business is locally owned and passionate about craftsmanship and community. Your commitment to creating an environment that values your work and this city is inspirational. I admire how the culture here emphasizes maintaining a healthy work-life balance while promoting hard work and creating a family dynamic that inspires collaboration. As a firm believer in teamwork and developing new and creative solutions through collaboration, I would be a valuable addition to this team.

"You've got to dance like nobody is watching, love as you'll never be hurt, sing like nobody is listening, and live like heaven is on earth."

E2 What Makes You Unique?

It's a beauty of creation that no man has an exact copy. Each of us is unique, just like each moment in time, every drop of rain, or every leaf on a tree. But it needs an eye of a romantic to spot the subtle differences around us and inside of us. When asking the question, most hiring managers and recruiters hope to hear about some unique skill, ability, personality trait, or experience that sets you apart from other job candidates. Last but not least, as I've already said, each of us is a unique living creature and will remain so until the end of time,

Sample 1

I would say that I possess a rare combination of high IQ and strong emotional intelligence. I can solve complex problems and work on complicated coding tasks, staying focused for hours. However, I do not live in a small bubble of my work desk. On the contrary, I can quickly identify when something is wrong with my colleagues and offer them a word of encouragement or a helping hand without hesitation. This is a rare combination, and I honestly believe it makes me unique, especially among programmers.

Sample 2

My natural ability to organize effectively is what sets me apart. In my previous role as an administrative assistant, I created a plan to reorganize the office supply closet by category. This made it easier to find items, so we placed fewer orders, ultimately saving 30% on office supplies year-over-year.

Sample 3

I'd say that my attitude to other people makes me a unique colleague. I am interested in my coworkers' feelings and emotions and try my best to bring positive energy and enthusiasm to the office.

In my experience, most corporations and teams will never reach their full potential because pointless internal conflicts hinder their growth. Colleagues are competing instead of cooperating.

You can be sure something like that won't happen when you have me on a team. I do not say that I am the only one with such an attitude, but judging by my experience, it is quite a rare one.

Sample 4

My ability to easily empathize with and relate to people makes me unique. This skill helped me in my previous role as an account executive in prospecting new accounts. Because I quickly identified and understood their pain points and challenges, I established a level of trust, which drove me to exceed my quota consistently. Unlike most people who seek recognition from their peers, I don't crave the validation of others' opinions.

Sample 5

My individuality makes me a unique being in this vast world. We all have unique gifts, but how we manage to translate those gifts into actual results and make a positive impact in the workplace sets us apart. I strive to use my talents to benefit others, but I don't consider myself successful because of it or better than other people. I don't boast about my achievements to gain social status; I believe that would be a trap I don't want to fall into. Perhaps my mindset makes me unique in that way.

Sample 6

In my opinion, every job seeker is unique. We have our own life stories, education, experiences, and relationships, including heartbreaks.

I try to stay humble, and instead of considering myself superior to my peers or other job applicants, I consider myself different.

I have a lot to offer, as you can see on my resume, as we've discussed here. However, instead of boasting about my skills, I prefer to stay humble and continuously work on proving myself.

That's how I see it. And I believe this mindset makes me unique.

Sample 7

What makes me unique is my four years of experience in retail. Because of my firsthand experience fielding shoppers' questions, feedback, and complaints, I deeply understand what customers want. I know what it takes to create a positive consumer experience through marketing.

Honestly, I do not care what others think of me and do not try to stand out in the crowd. I have my internal standards, and I know what I am capable of as a manager and what I can do for my employer.

Sample 8

My experience makes me unique, at least I think so. I have worked for two of your biggest competitors and know their business processes. I have connections in every institution involved in this business, including governmental agencies, and I believe you can benefit from my experience.

Everything I have done over the last seven years was with one goal in mind to get this same job with your company. You can be 100% sure that if I had the opportunity to work here, I would do my best day in and day out to stay with the company for many years.

"We are what we repeatedly do. Excellence, then, is not an act but a habit."

F 1 What Are Your Career Goals?

The idea is to break down large goals into smaller bite-size pieces. As you organize the steps and schedule your intentions for each milestone, you'll be amazed to see how much easier they are to reach. Foreseeing the future is equally important as staying in the present, working hard, and taking steps to reach your goals. The interviewer wants to know your career goals and where you want to head in the coming years.

Every long-term goal must be an ordered set of short-term goals you can achieve soon. Talk about how you reached your vision by completing a couple of short-term goals. Don't forget to align your goals with your current job position and domain in the industry. Make your goals relevant, realistic, and achievable. Keep your answer focused on your final achievements and generalized goals. This allows you to maintain flexibility and learn more about the company and position you're applying for.

Sample 1

My immediate goal is to secure a position at a company like this one where I can continue to grow and improve personally and professionally. I enjoy challenges and look forward to opportunities where I can assume more responsibilities. Ultimately, I would like to move into management, focusing on strategy and development, and build a solid career in the long term.

I am improving my communication skills through continuing education programs outside of work. I am highly interested in leadership positions and understand that effective communication is critical. Although I am content as a team member, I am excited to take on minor leadership roles and gradually work my way up to a manager and team leader position.

I feel very fortunate to have been surrounded by managers and team leaders who have been generous with their knowledge, and I am eager for the opportunity to become a mentor for others in this field.

Sample 2

I have worked in this field for a few years and have established short-term and long-term goals. I have added a few points to these goals following a similar pattern.

I want to utilize all my skills for my short-term targets. In the past few years, I haven't been able to use my full potential. This job opportunity will allow me to test my skills to the fullest.

Regarding my long-term plans, I want to take up leadership responsibilities and manage a team for a specific task. While working on my long-term plans, achieving my short-term goals can pave the way for them.

I am confident that I can accomplish these objectives.

Sample 3

I have kept my short-term goals reasonably simple. While reviewing the job description for this position, I identified the goals necessary to achieve the required targets mentioned in the job description. I aim to deliver more than what is expected of me.

As for my long-term goal, I seek bigger targets to challenge myself continuously. I understand that bigger targets can be tough to achieve, and I need to prepare myself during these initial years to deliver the best outcomes. I am committed to working towards these principles.

Sample 4

My perspective on short-term and long-term goals is pretty straightforward. For my short-term goals, I want to learn multiple sets of skills and master them. I can achieve this by working on various tasks from different fields with an experienced team.

Once I feel efficient in multiple skills, my long-term goal comes into play. I want to be assigned different responsibilities that suit my broad range of skills. Producing results in different sectors can be a fruitful way to progress my career.

Sample 5

As a fresher, my short-term goals will be important to my career progression. While working, my targets relate to making a mark in this field. During the initial years, I have to gain knowledge and experience. This will help me shape my career path. My long-term plans are straightforward. I want to climb the ranks and perform my duties as a team leader, which will ignite my desire to work smartly.

Sample 6

I have worked in this field for a while and set up goals to test myself accordingly. My short-term targets remain basic, and I will work on the assigned tasks to yield the expected outcomes. The targets are apparent in the job description. Further, as I settle down here, I want to take on more decision-making roles,

I see myself involved in more significant responsibilities, making tough decisions that can benefit the organization. For mutual growth, I have to work with the experience I have accumulated over all these years.

Sample 7

My short-term goals are pretty simple. I want to settle down in the new work environment quickly. It is necessary to adapt to a new environment for better performance.

Apart from this, my long-term goals are to grow within the job. Progress is the key. I want to see myself extracting every single drop of experience as I move forward. These are not just goals but also guidelines that I have to follow. Ultimately, it can be advantageous for both this organization and me.

Sample 8

Regarding my goal to lead a finance team, I have always been fascinated by the intricacies of financial management and analysis. With my academic background in finance and accounting, I believe that I possess the knowledge and skills necessary to excel in this field. Moreover, I have also developed strong leadership qualities over the years through various projects and group assignments.

In addition to leading a finance team, I am particularly drawn to working collaboratively with teams like legal and procurement to streamline processes. My experience in business administration has given me an appreciation for the value of optimizing processes to improve efficiency, and I believe I can leverage this skill set to drive organizational success.

Finally, the requirement for organizational expertise in this role is particularly appealing to me. I have had the good fortune of working under some truly inspiring managers, and I believe I can leverage their leadership styles and techniques to become an effective manager myself. I hope to manage my team and drive positive organizational change within a few years.

Sample 9

As a writer, I am passionate about crafting compelling stories that resonate with audiences. In today's digital age, creating engaging content cannot be overstated, as it is one of the most effective ways to build brand awareness and customer loyalty. By continuing to develop my writing skills, I hope to help brands achieve this goal and establish themselves as thought leaders in their respective industries.

In addition to writing, I recognize the importance of public speaking in today's business world. Communicating ideas is essential to success, whether presenting to clients or delivering a keynote at a conference. As such, I have been actively seeking out public speaking opportunities to improve my communication skills and develop my ability to connect with audiences.

I believe that my combined writing and public speaking skill sets can be particularly valuable to your company. By leveraging these skills, I hope to help establish your company as a leader in the industry by creating engaging and informative content while effectively communicating your message to your target audience.

Sample 10

Objectives determine your growth in any field. I did not emphasize much on goals during my graduation years. But after a certain point, I understood how important it is to set up targets. Otherwise, I would be lost in the dark.

I have set up short-term goals to enlighten my path. Initially, I wanted to learn the basics of working in a corporate environment. It is important to know what is right and wrong, and this can take a while, but I have plenty of things to learn. As I work on this, I will gather skills and experiences.

Regarding my long-term objectives, I picture myself having grown in the field and dealing with clients at a higher level. This will enable me to stand firm on my ground in decision-making in the upcoming years.

"Don't quit yet. The most beautiful silver linings usually follow the worst moments. You must stay strong, keep your head up, and remain hopeful."

F 2 How Do You Plan To Achieve Your Career Goals?

First, make sure you can name career goals beyond getting hired. You want to show that you are a long-term thinker with ambition for your future. Ensure that your goals align with your knowledge about the role and the company. It's vital to demonstrate to the interviewer that there's a match between what you're looking for and what the employer seeks in an ideal candidate.

What sets apart a good answer from an exceptional one is a description of the active strategy and steps you're taking to achieve those goals, which also speaks to your motivation and call to action.

A handy approach to answering this question is to use the STAR technique. With this technique, you'll talk about a Situation (S) or Task (T), the Action you took (A), and the Results achieved (R). This will help shape your answer while composing one that's uniquely yours. The technique helps keep your answer focused so you don't stray off-topic or speak too long.

Review these sample responses, but tailor your answer to your unique professional background, accomplishments, and plans.

Sample 1

Setting goals is crucial to success in any field, and I realized this after graduation. I have identified short-term and long-term objectives to help me navigate my career path. In the short term, I plan to focus on learning the basics of working in a corporate environment, which includes understanding the right and wrong ways of doing things. This may take some time, but I am eager to learn and gain the necessary skills and experiences.

As I gain more experience, I aim to take on more challenging roles that involve dealing with clients on a higher level. This will require me to make more complex decisions, but I'm excited about honing my decision-making skills and becoming more adept at handling difficult situations.

I am committed to continually developing my skills and knowledge by taking relevant classes and participating in professional associations to achieve these goals. I'm particularly interested in the training opportunities offered by your company, and I would be eager to take advantage of any relevant courses or programs. I can contribute to your team and help your company achieve its goals with the proper training and support.

Sample 2

Over the next five years, my primary objective is to gain a deeper understanding of the stock market and develop a comprehensive list of clients. I understand that this will require significant effort and dedication, and I am committed to taking the necessary steps to achieve this goal. I plan to enroll in courses that will help me enhance my knowledge of the stock market, including courses on investment strategies, market analysis, and financial planning.

In addition to taking classes, I plan to become actively involved in professional associations related to the financial industry. I believe networking with other professionals in the field will help me gain new insights and perspectives, which will be invaluable as I build my client base.

My long-term goal is to start my investment firm. I am passionate about helping people achieve their financial goals, and I believe that starting my firm will allow me to do just that. However, I understand that this is a long-term goal, and I am focused on gaining the necessary experience and skills to be successful in this endeavor.

To achieve my long-term goal, gaining experience as an account manager with a large company like yours would be an excellent stepping stone. I am confident that I have the skills and dedication necessary to excel in this role, and I am excited about the prospect of learning from experienced professionals in the industry.

Sample 3

I have always had a passion for journalism, and my college degree in Journalism was the first step towards pursuing this career path. However, my interest lies specifically in business journalism. Not everything can be learned in a classroom, so I seek opportunities to gain more in-depth knowledge about this field.

To further my understanding of business journalism, I frequently consult with my senior colleagues on the team and marketing department members. Communicating with cross-functional teams strengthens relationships and enhances our collective knowledge.

Additionally, I plan to enroll in online courses on digital marketing. Leveraging the digital space is essential for any organization to establish a strong brand presence and achieve a better return on investment (RoI). By combining my journalism and digital marketing skills, I am confident that I can contribute to making the organization a leader in the industry.

Sample 4

I have been fascinated by two things since childhood, History, and journalism. During my college years, I realized I could incorporate both passions while writing my thesis. Although I graduated with a History Major, I knew it alone could not help me succeed or gain recognition.

Writing numerous papers during my college years exposed me to the nitty-gritty. Still, I also realized that to understand it completely, I needed to apply for internships with media houses to understand what goes on behind the scenes. To achieve my goal of being renowned in the field, I took online courses and started reading up on the intricacies of multimedia journalism.

Sample 4

When I first realized my passion for becoming a veterinary technician, it was driven by my love for animals. I started researching the field in high school, focusing on the subjects I knew would be necessary for my college experience. In college, I pursued veterinary science and actively sought opportunities to network and gain experience in the industry. I attended workshops, applied for jobs, and continued studying to expand my knowledge of veterinary science and stay current with industry developments.

I believe that my efforts have prepared me very well for a job in this position. However, I am always eager to learn more and further develop my skills. I understand that this field requires ongoing education and professional development. I am committed to continuing my education and staying up-to-date with industry trends and advancements.

As a veterinary technician, I aim to provide the best possible care for animals.

Sample 5

I realized my interest in accounting when I found math subjects and related topics easy to comprehend. During high school and college, I found accounting courses to be simpler than expected, which led me to prepare for a career in accounting early on by studying and attending peer meetings. Last year, I attended numerous career fairs, and I hope to secure an internship before graduation. My coursework and studies have provided me with enough knowledge and understanding of accounting that I am confident I can perform effectively in the position once I become a full-time employee.

Sample 6

In college, I realized almost two years into my English degree that I love computer science. Although switching majors would set my education back one year, I decided to pursue my passion for computer science. I found the subject far more beneficial and interesting than what I was studying.

Throughout my courses, I collaborated with professors and other students to create personal projects such as games, visual novels, and other simple programs to test my abilities as a game developer. These experiences helped me gain hands-on experience and a deeper understanding of game development.

Now, in my senior year with one indie game nearly completed, I feel confident in my skills and believe I am well-prepared to enter the video game industry as a game developer. I am excited to continue learning and growing in this field and contribute to creating innovative and engaging games.

Sample 7

My education has been a strong foundation for achieving my career goals. During college, I worked hard to maintain a high GPA and was proud to graduate summa cum laude. This experience demonstrated my dedication and hard work and helped me develop time management and study skills that I know will be useful in any future role.

In addition to my academic achievements, I gained real-world experience through an internship with a publishing company last spring. During this time, I was able to work with experienced professionals in the industry and learn firsthand about the publishing process. This experience was invaluable, and I am grateful for the chance to apply the skills and knowledge I gained in my future career.

While I am confident in my abilities and experience, I understand there is always room for growth and development. That is why I am excited about the prospect of working as a full-time assistant, where I will have the chance to gain even more experience within the field. I am eager to take on new challenges and responsibilities and continue learning and growing professionally.

"Don't dream about success. Get out there and work for it."

G 1 What Are Your Hobbies

Cultivating a hobby shows dedication and passion toward something you love and can significantly boost your chances of getting hired. If possible, connect your hobby to the company or job. This will show your deep interest in the industry. For example, if you are applying for a job in gaming, you might mention your passion for certain video games. Remember that partying, gambling, and clubbing are not the right hobbies to bring up in an interview. Think of a productive hobby and discuss how you have cultivated the same over the years.

Be honest, but be careful not to go into so much detail about your hobbies that they will seem to threaten your commitment to the job. Research the company and see if your hobbies or interests fit the company culture. Keep your answers brief.

Sample 1

One of my hobbies is working out. I noticed in your job advertisement that you have a gym for your employees, which is attractive to me. Not only would I be able to work out there, but I would also have the opportunity to meet other employees in the gym and get to know them on a more casual basis.

Sample 2

One of my extracurricular activities is keeping up with my professional development and continuing education responsibilities. As you know, we must complete six hours of continuing education each year. To stay up-to-date in my area of expertise, I read professional journals, attend seminars, and occasionally take classes online or in a traditional classroom setting. Additionally, I often serve as one of the officers for our professional association.

Sample 3

I enjoy volunteer work and participating in community activities. Currently, I am coaching my son's Little League baseball team. In addition, I volunteer a couple of hours each week at a social services organization that distributes clothes and furnishings to people experiencing homelessness.

Sample 4

I have a variety of hobbies. I hike with my dog every chance I get. I spend time with my spouse and children. I try to work on the Telegraph crossword puzzle every weekend. I like to cook.

Sample 5

Since high school, I have always been passionate about baking and find time to do it every week. Every weekend, I try out new recipes, and the aroma that fills my kitchen while baking helps me de-stress.

In addition to baking, I have developed a habit of attending martial arts classes to stay fit. Not only has it made me stronger, but it has also improved my concentration levels, thereby increasing my productivity.

Sample 6

I enjoy playing sports like football and cricket and have represented my school and college in state and national-level tournaments. I honestly believe that my happy hormones are activated every time I am on the playing field. Once I discovered sports' effect on me, it was tough to give up. I still play 5-a-side football at least three times a week at the local club, and I look forward to these evenings with my team. Playing sports helps me stay fit both physically and mentally.

Additionally, I am the captain of the official cricket team at my present organization. You can check pictures of me and my teams on my social media handle.

Sample 7

During my school days, I was overly focused on academics and hardly ever took the time to develop any hobbies. However, I eventually decided to explore different hobbies and find one I truly enjoyed. I tried to learn string instruments like the violin and the guitar in this quest but didn't enjoy them. I can assure you that my roommates were the happiest when I put these instruments down! Eventually, I realized that I enjoyed traveling the most.

Yes I am a wanderlust. Visiting new places, exploring new roads, trying new cuisines, and learning about new cultures truly enthuse me! I dream of visiting all countries before I turn 50!

Sample 8

There are two activities that I am fond of yoga and crochet. My grandmother was my first crochet teacher and was excellent at handiwork. Crocheting is a meditative activity, and embracing it has dramatically enhanced my concentration.

As far as yoga is concerned, I started attending yoga classes a year ago at the insistence of a friend, and I have never looked back! In our industry, we have to interact with many people daily and spend most of our time outdoors. However, my hobbies help me connect with my inner self and allow me to spend some much-needed time indoors. Through these activities, I achieve balance and thoroughly enjoy my 'me' time.

Sample 9

I love to write in my free time, and I have tons of notebooks filled with plots, character sketches, and some random doodles. This passion was born during my childhood. Every summer, my parents would encourage my brothers and me to perform a skit. We would all find the perfect story, stitch our costumes, put up a set, and even make invitations! It was an elaborate affair and a fascinating experience.

Even back then, I loved being on the story and concept team. I take delight in writing short stories about the experiences I encounter every day. Due to my inclination towards writing and acting, I was a key member of the dramatics society during my school and college days.

I enjoy reading blogs and poetry.

Sample 10

I am highly influenced by art; my favorite painter is Vincent Van Gogh. His artwork inspires me, and I admire his painting style. Unfortunately, I cannot afford any of his original pieces, but fortunately, I have taken to making imitations of the paintings I sincerely love.

I only need a canvas, paints, and free time to study these paintings online. I have also learned about different eras and events from the history behind many of Van Gogh's artworks. When I started three years ago, I was only interested in painting imitations. I began by purchasing some DIY paint-by-number kits online, which are very popular globally because they are easy to complete, and even a school student can create a masterpiece with this kit. Eventually, I moved on to copying artwork from scratch as a hobby.

I also paint my imagination on canvas with watercolors and oil paints. This hobby has had a calming and liberating effect on me.

“The question isn’t who’s going to let me; it’s who’s going to stop me.”

G 2 What Is Your Dream Job?

While your skills are a key part of landing the job you want, your values also play a significant role in showing how the position you're interviewing for fits into your goals for the future. **Say something like:** Because of my passion for digital platforms; I want to be involved in working on projects like the ones your company is working on, especially because I love working in places that put an emphasis on collaborative environments and teamwork.

It would help if you also talked about what you can learn from this role and how this will help shape your career path within the industry. Be sure to mention that you're interested in the position for the long term. This will show employers you're committed to them and will stick around.

My dream job is to one day be a lead product manager, creating and scaling innovative tech products. Because of my passion for digital platforms, I want to be involved in working on projects like the ones your company is working on, mainly because I love working in places that put an emphasis on collaborative environments and teamwork. Being a Lead PM is a big goal, so I'm ready to do everything possible to develop my skills and work alongside talented people.

Answering What's your dream job? , is a great chance to show the interviewer that you're ambitious and forward-thinking and have the skills and values that will make you a great employee. By highlighting your great qualities and giving a thoughtful answer about how the position you're interviewing for will help you achieve your long-term goals, you'll impress the interviewer and get one step closer to landing the job.

Sample 1

As someone passionate about programming and product development, I have always enjoyed creating innovative and practical solutions to complex problems. However, I also believe that my skills and knowledge can be leveraged to make a meaningful impact on the society in which I live.

Therefore, my ultimate goal is to use my expertise to develop products that not only fulfill market demands but also contribute to the betterment of the community. I believe that by creating solutions that address social and environmental challenges, we can help society move forward and create a more equitable and sustainable future.

This would be my ultimate dream job: to combine my passion for technology with my desire to give back to society. I am excited by the possibilities and am committed to pursuing this path with determination and enthusiasm.

Sample 2

My dream job would be an opportunity to connect with people through my work and to make a positive impact in the industry. I aspire to leave my mark by creating products that solve real-world problems and benefit society.

I want to use my skills and expertise to make a meaningful contribution and to create solutions that have a lasting impact. Whether improving access to education, healthcare, or other essential services, technology can play a key role in addressing some of the world's most pressing challenges.

Ultimately, I want to be known for my innovation, creativity, and commitment to making a difference. I am driven by a passion for creating products that not only meet market demands but also make a positive impact on people's lives. This motivates me, and I am eager to pursue this goal with dedication and enthusiasm.

Sample 3

I aim to lead a team that significantly impacts our field through innovative and meaningful work. I am motivated by creating products that meet market demands, solve real-world problems, and improve people's lives.

I am excited to learn and grow professionally and am interested in joining your company. From what I have heard, your organization provides ample opportunities for growth and development, which is what I am looking for. Your company's continuous learning and improvement culture will enable me to achieve my goals and reach my full potential.

I am committed to fostering a collaborative and supportive work environment as a team leader. We can achieve great things together when the team feels empowered and motivated. I am eager to work alongside like-minded individuals who share my passion for technology and social impact.

My dream is to contribute to the advancement of the industry and create solutions that benefit society as a whole. Your company's values and vision align with mine, and I am excited about the prospect of working together to achieve our shared goals.

Sample 4

I pursued my medical degree with the hope and vision of helping people. However, after serving as a cardiologist in the industry, I realized that in India, access to medicine is a luxury afforded only by a few. This realization made me feel that I was not fulfilling my vision, and I understood that I lacked the necessary experience to make a real difference.

To gain the skills and knowledge necessary to achieve my vision, I pursued an MBA focusing on making generic medicine accessible to all. My dream job would be to work for a company that shares my belief in making affordable treatment available to those in need.

By doing so, we can help patients and enable doctors passionate about healing to make a greater impact. Everyone deserves access to quality healthcare, regardless of their economic situation, and I am dedicated to working towards this goal.

My vision is to be part of a movement that helps to transform the healthcare industry and create a more equitable society. I am committed to pursuing this vision with passion, dedication, and a spirit of collaboration.

Sample 5

I have always dreamed of being an editor in a leading media house, and I cannot think of a better company than yours. Although I know there is a long way to go, I am willing to try to achieve my dream. I am eager to start from the bottom as a sub-editor and work my way up the ladder. I believe that I will be able to do so under the mentorship of the great talents that your company already possesses.

Sample 6

My dream job involves working in a highly collaborative environment that emphasizes teamwork, where regular staff meetings and group projects are the norm. I am thrilled by the idea of working in a job that prioritizes communication among colleagues and encourages open dialogue between management and staff. In my previous job, I spent over 50% of my time working on team projects, and I am excited to continue that kind of teamwork and open communication here. Working together, we can achieve our shared goals and positively impact the company.

Sample 7

Since childhood, I have been fascinated with cartoons and video games, especially the creativity that goes into crafting unique and compelling characters. It didn't take me long to realize I wanted to pursue a career in this field. As I grew up, I became a huge admirer of (insert name of idol), who inspired me with their captivating work that left a lasting impression on me.

My dream job is to create designs that have a significant impact on the way people perceive things. I am eager to follow in the footsteps of my idol, using my creativity and skills to produce work of the same caliber. By creating memorable characters and designs, I hope to make a positive difference in people's lives and inspire future generations of artists and designers.

Sample 8

My dream job would involve developing web content for diverse companies, as I enjoy the challenge of tailoring content to meet each client's unique needs. In my previous job, I worked with clients from various industries, such as healthcare and education, and I received recognition for my ability to produce high-quality work for each of them.

The prospect of working with various clients from different fields excites me the most about this job. I am eager to learn about their products, services, and brand messaging and use my skills to create compelling content that resonates with their target audience. By doing so, I hope to contribute to their success and growth while expanding my skillset and knowledge in web content development.

Sample 9

I pursued engineering with the specific goal of making a difference in the renewable energy sector. Renewable energy resources are a crucial power source, and their use is key to solving many of the challenges modern-day India faces.

Therefore, my dream job would be to work with a company that shares my belief in the importance of renewable energy and is committed to creating a better future for the environment. I am eager to collaborate with like-minded professionals passionate about sustainability and possess the technical expertise to develop innovative solutions. I hope to create a cleaner, more sustainable future for all by working together towards this shared goal.

Sample 10

Since high school, I have held journalists and editors of media houses in high esteem. Their ability to effectively communicate news and craft compelling stories has always been a source of inspiration for me.

One of my aspirations since then has been to become a renowned editor, like my idol (insert name). I recognize that achieving such a status would require hard work, dedication, and learning from experienced colleagues in the field.

That's why I pursued journalism as a career, to hone my skills and develop my abilities in this field. I am eager to work alongside talented individuals and learn from their expertise to become a top-notch editor.

What draws me to this particular job is the opportunity to work for a company that shares my passion for journalism and storytelling. I am excited about contributing to a team that values excellence and delivers high-quality content to its readers. I am confident that my skills and experience align well with the job requirements, and I look forward to the chance to make a positive impact within this organization.

"You were meant to be here. This moment is yours."

H 1 What Type of Work Environment Do You Prefer?

You can only be at your maximum productivity if you are relaxed and feel that you fit in. When you are asked about work environments, your best bet is to try to stay relatively neutral at this stage in the interview process. Maintaining that you are flexible and adapt happily in any environment is a good idea.

How to speak at an interview about the work environment?

Research the employer before your interview to learn as much as possible about their work environment. Notice if this employer's environment seems casual or strict, more fast-paced or relaxed, etc.

When you describe the work environment you prefer, you want to make it sound like you'll excel in their environment, or else they're unlikely to hire you. So talk about how you do your best work in an environment like theirs. Please focus on the positive aspects and talk about why you work well in an environment like theirs instead of bad-mouthing or discussing why you dislike other work environments. It's always better to focus on the positives when describing the environment you work best in. Give specific examples if you can. For example, if this work environment is going to be very fast-paced, you'd want to tell them you do your best work in a fast-paced environment and then back it up with a real example of a past job in which you produced great work.

If there are specific environments that you absolutely cannot work in, do not say that you can handle them. For instance, if you are an accountant, you can say that you are flexible in terms of work environment but that you perform best when you have a relatively quiet space so you can drill into the numbers without distraction.

These examples of possible answers to this interview question may be helpful.

Sample 1

I am highly adaptable in my work environment and drawn to opportunities that challenge me to think creatively and work efficiently. After researching St. Jude's, Inc. on your website, I was impressed by the company's fast-paced and dynamic engineering department, which is geared towards expanding production and driving innovation.

I thrive in environments experiencing rapid growth and change, as such environments encourage new ideas and unique applications. Furthermore, I appreciate structure and organization, and I believe the engineering department at St. Jude's, Inc. aligns well with my work style and career goals.

I am excited about possibly contributing my skills and expertise to such an innovative company and working alongside talented professionals. I am confident that my abilities would enable me to make valuable contributions to the company's engineering department while furthering my professional growth and development.

Sample 2

Throughout my career, I have had the opportunity to work in a variety of company sizes, from small businesses to Fortune 500 firms. While I don't have a specific preference for company size, I have found that I excel in environments that foster collaboration and teamwork.

I genuinely enjoy working as part of a team, leveraging each person's unique skills and strengths to achieve a common goal. That being said, I am also capable of working independently when needed.

When I came across the job description for this role, I was immediately drawn to the emphasis on collaboration and cross-functional teamwork. In my previous roles, I found that effective communication and collaboration across teams and departments is crucial to success.

Given my background and strengths in these areas, I believe I would be an excellent fit for this role. I am excited about the possibility of working alongside a team of talented professionals and contributing to your organization's continued growth and success.

Sample 3

Having an energetic work environment can be a great motivating factor for many people. When employees are excited and enthusiastic about their work, it can create a positive atmosphere that increases productivity, creativity, and innovation.

Furthermore, when a company's culture values and encourages employee enthusiasm, it can help to retain valuable employees and attract top talent. Employees who feel appreciated and supported by their employers are more likely to stay with the company long-term, which can help to build a strong and stable workforce.

In my previous job, I worked for a company with a similar culture, and it was an environment where I felt comfortable and motivated to do my best work. It was a place where I could bounce ideas off my colleagues and work collaboratively to achieve our goals. This kind of environment helped me to learn new skills and develop professionally.

Overall, I believe that working in an energetic and positive environment is crucial for employee well-being, job satisfaction, and overall success in a job.

Sample 4

I have worked in various environments, including corporate offices, small businesses, and remote teams. Each experience has taught me something new and allowed me to develop my skills in different areas. However, I have found that I thrive when working alongside individuals who are dedicated to achieving their goals and passionate about their work.

For me, it's not just about the work environment itself but rather the people I work with. I appreciate those willing to put in the effort and drive to succeed. This kind of attitude is infectious and motivates me to be my best self. I also value working with individuals open to learning and growing, as I believe we can continuously improve our skills and knowledge.

I am adaptable and can work effectively in any environment if the people around me are motivated and committed. Working with a team of like-minded individuals can lead to great results, and I look forward to collaborating with passionate professionals in my next role.

Sample 5

The camaraderie among team members and a good work ethic are crucial factors that make a workplace enjoyable for me. When team members trust and support each other, I have found that it creates a positive and productive work environment.

I thrive when working with people who are competent, kind, and have a good sense of humor. A positive attitude and a willingness to have fun while working can contribute to a more relaxed and enjoyable workplace. At the same time, it's important that everyone takes their work seriously and is committed to achieving their goals.

One of my previous jobs was at a company where I had the opportunity to work with a team with all these qualities. We had a great working relationship and accomplished a lot together. It was a fun and productive environment, and I believe I can bring that same positive attitude and strong work ethic to any team I work with.

Sample 6

My ideal work environment is adaptive, meaning it can easily handle fast-paced work and is ready for challenges. It also knows how to slow down when work is slow, recognizing the natural shifts in business and responding accordingly. I believe it's important for a company to adapt to changing circumstances and remain flexible in its approach to work. This adaptability also requires open communication among team members and a willingness to learn from mistakes and adjust course as needed. I value a work environment where people are encouraged to speak up and share their ideas and where teamwork is emphasized. When everyone is working together towards a common goal, I find that we can achieve great things.

Sample 7

My ideal work environment provides both autonomy and collaboration. On the one hand, I value having dedicated time and space to focus on my work without interruptions or distractions. This could mean having a private workspace, working remotely, or having clear boundaries and expectations around when I am available for meetings or other interactions.

On the other hand, I also thrive in a collaborative environment where teamwork is encouraged and supported. However, this collaboration must be based on mutual respect and a shared goal rather than office politics or competition. I want to work with people who are supportive, communicative, and focused on achieving results as a team,

In summary, my ideal work environment balances autonomy and collaboration and is characterized by clear boundaries, mutual respect, and a shared focus on achieving success together.

Sample 8

I like the work environment in my current position. My manager is a great resource who is always willing to help when I encounter issues. They also trust me to get my work done, so I have a lot of freedom in how I schedule and prioritize my tasks, which is very important to me.,

In terms of the physical environment, everyone has their cubicle, so it's often pretty quiet, which helps me focus on my work. However, we all get lunch together, and our team has a lot of check-in meetings and frequent communication via Slack, so we still get a lot of opportunities to bounce ideas off each other and collaborate. I appreciate both individual and collaborative work, and I think my current workplace strikes a good balance between the two.

Sample 9

I have found that I tend to thrive more in collaborative work environments. I prefer a workplace where all team members' opinions and ideas are valued because I believe it leads to a better outcome for any project in the long run. That's why I also appreciate an open office concept, like the one you have here, where it's easy to check in with other team members, managers, or even individuals from other teams who can bring fresh perspectives or specialized expertise.

However, I also understand that there are times when I need to focus and work independently, and I appreciate the privacy rooms you pointed out during the tour. They can be very helpful in allowing me to concentrate and get things done after I have received the necessary input and collaboration from others.

"Opportunities don't happen. You create them."

H 2 Tell Me About Your Education

The best way to prepare to respond is to start with a careful examination of the key qualifications that your employer is seeking. Look for an essential qualification that corresponds well with one of your most prominent assets. Often employers list the skills they desire, and you can use those listed. This approach is beneficial if you have those additional skills but are lacking in some of the ones they mention.

Think of a situation in which you applied that strength to the advantage of your employer and be ready to share any positive results you generated. If possible, prepare two or three stories of how you have added value in different contexts by tapping that strength. Point out how that strength might be beneficial to the employer.

If you're unsure of your core strengths, now is a good time to figure them out before your interview. There are a few ways you can do this:

Ask someone: It's often hard to assess our strengths and weaknesses, but a friend or colleague you trust should be able to shed some light on the topic for you.

Check out LinkedIn: Browse the skills and endorsements on LinkedIn for people in similar roles to your own. The skills for which they are most highly endorsed are likely ones you have too.

Consider previous achievements and praise: When you've received feedback from your colleagues and managers, what has been said about your work? Whether the feedback came from a professor or a boss, it could be useful now in identifying your qualifications, abilities, and strong points.

Sample 1

Throughout my academic journey, I have always been eager to expand my knowledge beyond what was taught in the classroom. For instance, I was introduced to various programming languages during my computer software studies. However, I didn't want to limit myself to learning languages. Instead, I sought to apply my knowledge by creating mini-projects demonstrating my language understanding. This approach reinforced my theoretical knowledge and helped me gain practical experience.

Moreover, as I progressed through my studies, I became increasingly interested in emerging technologies such as Big Data and Machine Learning. To broaden my understanding of these fields, I enrolled in online courses and completed all relevant projects associated with the courses. Doing so gave me a wealth of practical knowledge to supplement my theoretical understanding.

In summary, my passion for learning extends beyond the confines of traditional education. I actively seek opportunities to enhance my knowledge and skills in theory and practice to make valuable contributions in any role I undertake.

Sample 2

My graduate education was in Communications and Journalism, where I gained valuable skills that have helped me excel in my career. The courses I took in this program taught me how to communicate with clients and colleagues effectively and helped me develop stronger business relationships through professional correspondence. Additionally, I learned persuasive writing skills, which have proven incredibly helpful when editing client proposals and crafting compelling pitches for potential clients. Through this program, I also honed my research skills, which have been useful in conducting market analysis and gathering information for client projects. Overall, my graduate education has equipped me with the skills and knowledge necessary to succeed in the fast-paced and constantly evolving field of communications and journalism.

Sample 3

I received my Master's degree in Computer Engineering and Computer Science in 2009, following my undergraduate degree in Computer Science. These invaluable educational experiences have helped me lay a strong foundation for building a successful career in the highly competitive and in-demand tech industry.

One area where I have particularly excelled is in Computer Science Project Management. My proficiency in this field has equipped me with the necessary skills and knowledge to take up leadership roles where I oversee teams of developers and engineers. With my abilities in project management and technical expertise, I am confident in my ability to lead teams toward successful project outcomes.

Sample 4

I completed my Business Degree with a major in Economics from Calcutta University. During my time there, I had the opportunity to participate in their international exchange program, which took me to Singapore for 12 weeks. This experience proved to be incredibly rewarding, both personally and professionally.

While my coursework focused primarily on macroeconomics and the global trading system, my time in Singapore also exposed me to different cultures and ways of communication. This experience taught me valuable soft skills such as cross-cultural communication and adaptability. In addition, I even picked up some basic conversational skills in Malay and Mandarin Chinese.

Aside from cultural exposure, the exchange program also helped me hone my time management and cross-collaboration skills. These are essential skills in any workplace, and I am confident they will serve me well in this new role. I also learned the importance of self-motivation, which has helped me to be more productive and efficient in my work.

Sample 5

I hold an Associate's Degree in Fashion Merchandising and a Bachelor's in Media and Communications. During my academic journey, I was recognized for my excellent grades and received a scholarship for my achievements. I also actively participated in various student body groups, which helped me to develop essential leadership and teamwork skills.

My education in Fashion Merchandising has proven invaluable in my current role. As a team member responsible for planning store displays, I can utilize my knowledge and expertise to create visually appealing and engaging displays that attract customers. My training in this field has also helped me develop innovative collections and campaigns that resonate with our target audience.

My Bachelor's Degree in Media and Communications has helped me to establish and maintain strong connections with customers, both online and in-person. I can leverage my expertise to create compelling social media campaigns and engaging content that helps to build brand awareness and foster engagement. Whether working alongside a customer or attending a local fashion event, I am confident I can contribute to achieving our critical goals. The knowledge and skills gained from my formal education have made me a versatile and valuable asset to my team.

Sample 6

I hold a Bachelor of Arts degree in English from St. Xavier, where I graduated with a score of 73%. Despite working full-time while pursuing my degree, I am proud of my achievement and the dedication and discipline it required. This experience taught me valuable time management skills, and I discovered that I work best under pressure.

My university education equipped me with essential communication skills instrumental in my career growth. Since graduating, I have continued to refine and expand upon these competencies. For example, I have honed my negotiation skills and built my confidence in public speaking through continued education and practice.

I am excited to join your company and work alongside your incredible team. I am confident that the knowledge and professional skills I have acquired through my formal education and work experience will enable me to contribute to achieving your company's goals.

Sample 7

In 2011, I completed my Bachelor of Education Degree from St. Joseph's University with honors and was on the Dean's list for three years. While at the University, I actively participated in competitive soccer and volleyball and proudly served as the volleyball team captain in my final year.

Currently, I am considering the idea of pursuing a Master of Education degree, which I can conveniently complete online through IGNOU. As a dedicated teacher, I prioritize continuous learning and strive to set an exceptional example for my high school students.

Sample 8

I hold a Master's Degree in Engineering specializing in Application Engineering, which I earned with academic distinction. Throughout my degree program, I discovered that my proficiency in mathematical modeling was particularly strong, leading me to achieve top grades in this field of study. As a result of my academic performance and dedication, I graduated at the top of my class and received numerous scholarships throughout my college career.

Sample 9

Along with my Bachelor's and Master's Degrees in Social Work, I have also committed extensive hours volunteering with our local Women's Shelter and nearby schools. For the past four years, I have worked alongside an incredible team of professionals, utilizing my expertise to provide necessary intervention and counseling services to families within their homes.

My dedication to community service and social work stems from a deep passion for advocating for vulnerable populations and fostering positive societal change. Through my volunteer work and professional experiences, I have gained valuable insights and skills that have enabled me to make a meaningful impact in the lives of those I serve.

"I never lose. Either I win, or I learn."

11 Are You A Team Player?

During job interviews, hiring managers often ask, Are you a team player? to assess your ability to collaborate, communicate effectively, and function well within a group setting. Essentially, they evaluate whether you would be a suitable candidate for the position and the organization's culture.

Being a team player is critical to any job, as it is essential for completing tasks efficiently and effectively. Collaborating with others can lead to new ideas, solutions, and approaches that may not have been possible working alone. Communication and interpersonal skills are crucial to building strong relationships with colleagues and working together towards common goals.

Therefore, when asked this question, it is important to demonstrate your willingness to work with others, highlight relevant examples of past collaborative experiences, and explain how you have contributed to team success in previous roles. By doing so, you can convey your value as a team player and demonstrate your potential as a valuable asset to the company.

Sample 1

Being a part of a team is something I find truly enjoyable, and I thrive when I can collaborate meaningfully and effectively. In my previous position, I had the opportunity to demonstrate my ability to work well within a team and contribute to its success.

One accomplishment I am proud of was developing and implementing procedures that streamlined communication among team members. By doing so, I facilitated a more cohesive and efficient working environment, leading to increased productivity and better results. My efforts were appreciated by my colleagues and superiors alike, as the team could complete tasks more efficiently and with greater accuracy.

This experience has reinforced my belief in the power of collaboration and teamwork, and I am excited to bring this mindset to any future positions I hold. We can achieve great things together by working closely with others and leveraging our strengths.

Sample 2

I am a team player, believing every great achievement results from a collaborative effort. I am fully aware that I could hardly achieve anything remarkable on my own, and I always strive to work closely with others to achieve our shared goals.

I am particularly drawn to your corporation due to its reputation for fostering an exceptional workplace atmosphere and promoting excellent cooperation within small teams and across departments. This is one of the main reasons I applied for a job with your company, as I believe I can thrive in such an environment.

I am eagerly looking forward to meeting my new colleagues, and I am confident that my unique perspective and experiences will contribute positively to the diversity of your team. By working together, I am certain that we can achieve great things and continue to build upon the impressive reputation of your corporation.

Sample 3

Throughout my career, I have had the opportunity to serve as both a team leader and contributor. I have gained a wealth of experience working effectively within a team environment. As a result, I am incredibly comfortable collaborating with others and contributing to team success.

No matter my role, I always strive to utilize my reliability, excellent communication skills, positive attitude, and outgoing personality to become a key contributor to the team. By being reliable, I ensure that my colleagues can count on me to deliver quality work and meet critical deadlines. Moreover, my strong communication skills enable me to effectively convey ideas and ensure everyone is on the same page. A positive attitude is essential in creating a supportive and collaborative working environment, and my outgoing personality allows me to establish positive relationships with my colleagues.

I am passionate about working in teams and excited to bring my skills and experience to your organization. I am confident that I can be a valuable asset to any team, and I look forward to contributing to your company's success.

Sample 4

Based on my extensive working experience, I firmly believe that I am a dedicated team player. In my previous role in retail, I had the privilege of being part of an exceptional team of sales employees. We collaborated closely, constantly supporting and encouraging each other, which made working together an enjoyable experience.

We achieved outstanding results thanks to our collective efforts, reinforcing my conviction that teamwork is essential to success in any field. I am proud of my role in contributing to our team's success, and I firmly believe that my ability to work well with others is a key strength that I can bring to any organization.

I am eager to continue working in a team environment where I can apply my strong collaboration skills, positive attitude, and work ethic to help achieve shared goals. I am confident that my experience and approach to teamwork will make me a valuable asset to any organization.

Sample 5

I wholeheartedly believe that teamwork is essential to any successful engineering project. While technical skills are undoubtedly critical to the field, effective collaboration sets the most successful engineers apart.

I have strongly emphasized teamwork throughout my career, recognizing that it takes a collaborative effort to succeed in the engineering industry. In my previous role, I was able to leverage my collaboration skills to great effect, earning praise from my supervisor for my ability to communicate with my team effectively. We worked together to cultivate creative solutions to complex problems, and I was able to explain these solutions clearly to colleagues in marketing and sales who may have lacked technical knowledge.

I am passionate about working collaboratively with others, recognizing the value that diverse perspectives and skill sets bring to any project. I believe that my experience in fostering positive working relationships with team members of various backgrounds and skill levels will enable me to make valuable contributions to any engineering team.

I am eager to bring my skills and experience to your organization, and I am confident that my approach to teamwork will allow me to excel in the engineering field.

Sample 6

I prefer to take responsibility for my work and thrive when given a sense of ownership over my tasks. In my previous job at a large electronics store, I found that some of my colleagues lacked motivation and didn't take responsibility for their work. I had to pick up the slack and do extra work to ensure our team met our goals. While this wasn't ideal, I could step up and ensure that the team's performance didn't suffer due to my colleagues' lack of motivation.

I am excited about the prospect of working for your company, as I understand that your store operates with only one person on each shift. This model suits me perfectly, as I am comfortable working independently and solely responsible for the store's daily operations and sales. I believe that my strong work ethic and ability to take ownership of my work will allow me to excel in this role and contribute to the success of your business.

Sample 7

My approach to teamwork varies depending on the situation. Generally speaking, I do enjoy being a team player and supporting my colleagues. However, sometimes I feel it's necessary to speak up and stand for what I believe is right. For example, if I notice an ethical issue or disagree with a certain policy, I don't hesitate to voice my concerns and take action.

I think it's important to have strong values and not just blindly follow the rest of the team. At the same time, I understand the value of collaboration and compromise, and I'm always willing to work with my team to find a solution that everyone can agree on. A balance between independent thinking and teamwork is essential for organizational success.

Sample 8

I have been a team player throughout my life, and I find it incredibly fulfilling to share a common vision or passion with others. Additionally, I am willing to make sacrifices for the team's betterment. In my previous job, there was a time when we had to push for a new design, and I was the only team member who did not have family commitments. Therefore, I willingly stayed overtime for ten consecutive days, working tirelessly on the design. It was a small sacrifice on my part, but it was worth it to contribute to the team's success.

"Doubt kills more dreams than failure ever will."

12 Are You A Leader or A Follower?

Everyone can boast about their leadership skills, especially during a job interview when interacting with individuals they have never met. However, true strength lies in acknowledging and accepting one's weaknesses.

Individuals who remain humble, and refrain from considering their subordinates inferior or unintelligent, are the epitome of great leaders. Managers who are open to receiving feedback from their subordinates or followers and continually strive to innovate themselves are the ones who lead companies and teams to success.

It is crucial to understand that a leader's primary role is to motivate and inspire their team to achieve their goals. It is impossible to accomplish this feat without acknowledging the areas that require improvement. Great leaders are not afraid to admit their shortcomings and work towards overcoming them.

This ability to remain humble and receptive to constructive criticism is a sign of a great leader. Such individuals set an example for their team members and create an environment of mutual trust and respect. They empower their subordinates to speak up and share their opinions without fear of retaliation. Consequently, a company or team led by such a leader will likely succeed in the long run.

Sample 1

I would certainly describe myself as a leader, as I possess several key leadership qualities. I am proactive, always willing to take the initiative and suggest innovative ideas. Furthermore, I strongly believe in leading by example. This has been demonstrated in various situations during my previous employment.

For instance, I consciously decided to arrive at work at 7 am, earlier than the regular start time. My primary motivation was to have more time to work on various projects and leave the office earlier in the afternoon. Initially, many of my colleagues thought I was crazy for doing so. However, as they observed my productivity, which was excellent, and saw that I was able to leave the office by 3:30 pm, some of them began to follow my example and also started arriving at work at 7 am.

This illustrates that I am not afraid to take risks and try new approaches, even if it goes against the norm. I can inspire others to adopt similar practices, leading to a more efficient and productive workplace.

In addition to leading by example, I possess excellent communication and interpersonal skills, which are crucial in any leadership role. I am always willing to listen to others and consider their opinions. Moreover, I strive to create a collaborative environment where everyone feels valued and respected, which can foster creativity and innovation.

My leadership qualities, such as proactiveness, innovation, leading by example, excellent communication, and interpersonal skills, make me a strong candidate for any leadership role.

Sample 2

I have primarily been a follower throughout my life so far. I have always tried to learn from individuals with more experience than me, observing how they work and lead their teams. However, I have reached a point where I aspire to become a leader. Ideally, I would like to transition now, as I believe I have accumulated enough knowledge and experience to form my opinions and attitudes. Moreover, I can offer valuable insights and guidance to those who follow my leadership.

As a follower, I have learned much about the qualities of a good leader. I have observed how great leaders communicate, motivate, and inspire their teams to achieve common goals. I have also observed how leaders handle difficult situations, navigate complex problems, and foster a collaborative work environment.

Having gathered all this information and experience, I am eager to take on a leadership role. I am confident in my ability to develop and implement successful strategies, effectively communicate with team members, and inspire them to work towards achieving our collective objectives.

I understand that being a leader also entails being a good listener and taking into account the perspectives and opinions of others. I am open to constructive feedback and believe that it is crucial in ensuring the growth and success of both myself and my team.

While I may have been a follower in the past, I am now ready to take on the responsibilities of a leader. I have the necessary skills and experience and am eager to guide and support those who follow my leadership.

Sample 3

I cannot pinpoint why, but people have consistently looked up to me as a role model. Perhaps it's due to my imposing stature, being quite tall and big overall. Or maybe it's because of my unwavering commitment to excel in everything I do. This mindset drives me to give 100% to every activity I undertake, or else I don't bother doing it. This attitude may inspire people around me, prompting them to follow my lead and seek my advice when they face difficulties. While this is my impression, to truly comprehend what draws people to my leadership, it would be best to ask them directly.

Regardless, my natural leadership qualities have also played a significant role in inspiring others. I possess excellent communication skills and can convey my thoughts and ideas clearly and effectively. I am also attentive and empathetic, always willing to listen and support those in need. Additionally, I believe in leading by example and consistently demonstrating the behaviors and work ethic I expect from others.

Through these attributes, I have established myself as a reliable individual, someone others can admire and trust. I genuinely desire to help others succeed and thrive and derive immense satisfaction from seeing those around me grow and develop. As a leader, I aim to create a positive, inclusive work environment fostering collaboration and innovation.

While I may not be certain why people follow my example, I believe that my attributes, such as my unwavering commitment to excellence, effective communication skills, empathy, and leading by example, have all played a part. I am grateful for the trust and support that others have bestowed upon me, and I will continue to strive to be the best leader I can be.

Sample 4

Regarding leadership, I consider myself a leader and a follower. On the one hand, I am not afraid to lead by example and express my opinions, even to those who are more experienced than I am. A leader must be willing to take risks and make difficult decisions, even if it means challenging the status quo.

On the other hand, I remain humble and recognize that there is always more to learn. I do not see myself as superior to my colleagues or subordinates but as a collaborator who can learn from their unique perspectives and experiences. I am open to feedback and strive to improve my skills and knowledge.

I believe that a great leader is someone who can strike a balance between confidence and humility. While taking charge and inspiring others is essential, listening and learning from those around you is also crucial. By fostering a collaborative and inclusive work environment, I can ensure that everyone has the opportunity to contribute to our shared success.

Building a strong relationship with my colleagues and subordinates is essential based on trust and respect. By treating everyone with dignity and valuing their contributions, I can create a positive work culture that encourages innovation and creativity.

My leadership style is a blend of leading by example and being receptive to feedback and collaboration. By maintaining a balance between these two approaches, I can create a positive and inclusive work environment where everyone has the opportunity to thrive and succeed.

Sample 5

I recall a time from my previous role as a call center manager that exemplified my leadership skills. It was the end of 2019, and our sales were declining. Some employees had left abruptly, and the overall morale in the workplace was low.

I decided to take action to address the situation. I spoke with each employee, offering encouragement and support during the challenging period. I also developed new sales strategies for making cold calls and even implemented them to show that I was willing to lead by example and put my ideas into practice.

Through perseverance and determination, we overcame the difficulties, and the call center ultimately emerged stronger. While I am no longer with the company, this experience demonstrated my ability to lead even in challenging times.

As a leader, I believe it is essential to remain steadfast and optimistic, even when things are tough. A leader can inspire others to rise to the occasion and work towards a common goal by staying engaged with the team and actively addressing the challenges.

Leading with empathy and understanding is crucial, recognizing that every employee has unique circumstances and challenges. By taking the time to listen and offer support, a leader can foster a sense of trust and collaboration, leading to greater success for the team.

My experience in the call center demonstrated my leadership abilities, particularly in challenging times. By taking an active role in addressing the issues, leading by example, and remaining optimistic and empathetic, I was able to guide the team toward success.

Sample 6

I have always been fascinated by the field of business and management. I believe that effective leadership is essential for the success of any organization, and I am passionate about developing the skills and knowledge necessary to become an exceptional leader.

One experience that stands out to me as a defining moment in my pursuit of leadership was my time as a project manager for a marketing campaign. I led a team of designers, writers, and marketing specialists, all with unique skill sets and perspectives.

At the outset of the project, I realized that I needed to establish clear goals and expectations for the team. I met with each team member individually to get to know them and understand their strengths and weaknesses. From there, I set goals and deadlines that were challenging yet achievable, ensuring that each team member had a clear understanding of their role and responsibilities.

Throughout the project, I remained highly engaged with the team, providing guidance and support as needed and fostering an environment of open communication and collaboration. I encouraged team members to share their ideas and perspectives and was always open to feedback and constructive criticism.

Ultimately, the project was a great success, exceeding our initial goals and expectations. This experience reinforced my belief in the power of effective leadership and motivated me to continue pursuing opportunities to develop my skills in this area.

I am excited to hone my leadership abilities further and positively impact the organizations and teams I work with. Leadership is about achieving success and inspiring and empowering others to reach their full potential. With dedication, hard work, and a commitment to continuous learning, I am confident that I can become the kind of leader others look up to and respect.

Sample 7

Indeed, leadership skills are essential in any field. As a leader, you must communicate effectively, motivate your team, and take responsibility for your actions. In my previous job, I was in charge of a team of graphic designers. One of the best examples of my leadership skills was when a major project was due, and we were behind schedule. The team was feeling the pressure, and morale was low.

To tackle this challenge, I held a team meeting where I listened to everyone's concerns and ideas, and we devised a plan to get back on track. I delegated specific tasks to each team member based on their strengths and experience, and I communicated clearly and regularly with the team about our progress.

I also tried to boost morale by organizing team-building activities and recognizing each team member's hard work and achievements. This combination of clear communication, delegation, and motivation helped us complete the project on time and strengthened the bond between team members.

My experience leading a graphic design team showed me the importance of being a supportive and effective leader. By taking the time to listen, communicate, and motivate, I was able to help my team achieve their goals and feel valued in the workplace.

"Work hard, be kind, and amazing things will happen."

J 1 Why Should We Hire You?

You never know what other candidates can offer the company, but you know yourself. Emphasize your key skills, strengths, talents, work experience, and professional achievements fundamental to accomplishing great things in this position. Be honest with both yourself and your prospective employer. You won't make it far if you lie. Being called for an interview means they believe in your capabilities.

Apart from highlighting your skills and experience, show your enthusiasm to prove that you'll have a positive attitude towards your tasks. Demonstrate corresponding personal and professional traits that make you a great addition to the team. Identify the company's culture, department characteristics, company goals, and how your specific skills and experience can be useful. Emphasize your uniqueness, but keep it concise. Highlight your strengths, skills, and accomplishments. Give an example that describes you as a quick learner. State or provide evidence of how you contributed to the growth of your previous company in terms of revenue, goodwill, and brand. Include the research you have conducted on the company. For smaller companies (2 to 50 employees), you can say, Your company is open to new innovative ideas.

Avoid saying, I need a job, money, or This place is close to where I live. Focus on what you can do for the company rather than what they can do for you. Never compare your skills to others. The instinct when asked this question is to start comparing our skills to others, but it's best to avoid this.

Sample 1

Over the years, I have acquired a wide range of relevant skills and valuable experience that I am confident will benefit your organization. Additionally, I have dedicated considerable time and effort to improving my communication and teamwork skills, which I believe are essential for success in any professional setting. If given the opportunity to join your team, I am eager to apply these skills and knowledge to help drive the organization forward.

Through my previous work experiences, I have learned the importance of giving my all and striving for excellence in all that I do. By doing so, I have gained a deeper understanding of my capabilities and limitations and how to leverage them effectively to achieve the best possible outcomes. Moving forward, I am excited to continue this approach in my future career, particularly in your esteemed organization, where I am confident I can make a meaningful contribution.

My skills, experience, and work ethic make me an ideal candidate. If selected, I am eager to work collaboratively with my colleagues and contribute to the organization's success in any way possible.

Sample 2

For this particular job, I possess an ideal blend of skills and experience required for the role. I have honed my abilities through various work experiences and academic pursuits, making me a strong fit for this position. Moreover, my exposure to diverse working environments and situations has helped me develop strong analytical and problem-solving skills. I have used these skills to identify potential issues and devise solutions that have contributed to the growth and success of previous organizations I have worked for.

I am confident that my dedication to maintaining high work standards will be a valuable addition to the team and the company. In my previous roles, I have always strived to deliver quality work, pay attention to details, and meet project timelines. I understand the importance of teamwork and communication to achieve desired results. Therefore, I am committed to fostering positive working relationships with colleagues, managers, and stakeholders to ensure we work together towards a common goal.

My skills, experience, and work ethic make me an excellent fit for this job.

Sample 3

I am thrilled to work with a recognized brand for its excellence and accomplishments. As a fresher, I am excited to start my career in such a prestigious organization that will provide me with an excellent platform to learn and grow my skills and knowledge in the corporate world. I am confident that I possess the right attitude, dedication, and commitment to perform to the best of my abilities and contribute to the growth and welfare of this great brand. With my eagerness to learn and willingness to work hard, I can make a significant difference in the team and the company. Thank you for considering my application and giving me a chance to showcase my potential.

Sample 4

I am well-versed in your company's mission to acquire the largest consumer base in the area and become a leading provider in the community. With my extensive domain knowledge and experience in handling customers, I firmly believe I can significantly contribute to achieving this goal. I am confident that my expertise and insights can help the company grow and expand its reach in the market.

I am excited by the prospect of taking on this challenge and helping to build this business further. My passion for customer service and ability to create strong client relationships can help the company attract and retain customers. As someone dedicated to excellence, I work tirelessly to meet and exceed the company's expectations.

I look forward to demonstrating my capabilities and contributing to the company's success.

Sample 5

I possess all the skills and experience you are looking for, and I am confident I am the best candidate for this job. My past project background and people skills make me an ideal fit for this position.

I am self-motivated and strive to exceed my superior's expectations with high-quality work. I have a knack for quickly picking up business knowledge related to my project, making me a fast learner.

Lastly, I would like to add that I excel as an individual contributor and a team member. I firmly believe that my collaborative approach to work and my ability to work seamlessly with others make me an ideal candidate for this role.

These skills and experiences make me a complete package for this job, and I am excited about the opportunity to contribute to your organization.

Sample 6

I am confident that I possess the necessary skills and training that you are seeking in an editorial assistant. I have gained a strong foundational knowledge of the editing and professional process with my previous experience as the chief editor for my college magazine for two years. Working on the magazine also helped me build a diverse skill set, including excellent communication and interpersonal skills, as I regularly interacted with faculty and students.

My passion for publishing has grown stronger with time, and I am committed to delivering high-quality work to the best of my abilities. I am well-versed in using different editing software and tools and have a keen eye for detail, which is essential for proofreading and copyediting. Additionally, I have excellent organizational skills and can multitask effectively, enabling me to manage multiple projects simultaneously.

As an editorial assistant, I am excited to be part of a team that strives for excellence in the publishing industry. I am willing to learn and adapt to the company's working style and ethos, and I believe my dedication and passion will make me a valuable asset to your team.

Sample 7

I have had the privilege of working as a Software Tester with esteemed organizations like TCS and HCL Technologies, which has provided me with valuable firsthand experience in the field of testing. During my past career, I had the opportunity to lead several critical manual and automated software testing projects, which helped me gain a holistic view of the work front. As a result, I received certificates for my exemplary project management skills.

I possess about five years of experience in the domain, which has given me ample time to grow and gain expertise in people management in a reputed company like yours. I believe that your organization would be the perfect place for me to continue developing my skills in my preferred domain. I am confident that I can contribute positively to the team and help take the company to new heights with my technical and leadership abilities.

Sample 8

As a fresher, I am adaptable and eager to learn new things. I am confident that I will be able to make a valuable contribution to the development of your organization. My previous experience in Operations has taught me the importance of being a cooperative team player, and I am confident that this quality will be a valuable asset in any role I take on. I am committed to following organizational rules and procedures and will always strive to follow the rulebook.

Although I do not have any prior work experience or extensive knowledge in the field, I am confident that with hard work and dedication, I will be able to learn quickly and effectively. In school, I was an excellent speaker and made many friends. My strong communication skills will enable me to be an effective digital marketing manager. I am also very hardworking and a fast learner, which will allow me to shape myself into the ideal candidate for the position.

I am confident that I have the potential to excel in the role of a digital marketing manager. With my strong work ethic, dedication to learning, and excellent communication skills, I am sure that I can positively contribute to your organization and help drive its growth and success.

Sample 9

I am confident that my exceptional communication skills will make me a valuable asset to your organization. I actively participated in debates and public speaking competitions during college, which helped me hone my communication skills. Though I may not have any prior work experience in digital marketing, I am willing to put in the time and effort to learn and excel in this role. I believe that with my hard-working nature and quick learning abilities, I can quickly adapt to the requirements of this role and deliver quality work.

My ability to understand and implement processes will be beneficial in executing digital marketing strategies. I have a strong grasping quality, and I am confident I can quickly comprehend and execute any new process or strategy related to this domain.

I am excited about the opportunity to join your team as a digital marketing executive and contribute to the growth and success of your organization.

Sample 10

As someone with around five years of experience in various types of writing, I believe I am well-suited for this position. Over the years, I have honed my writing skills and gained expertise in writing for news magazines, creating web content, and editing documents for the study abroad industry. This has allowed me to develop a diverse skill set perfect for a company like yours that values creativity.

After taking the written test, I saw that my writing style aligns with your company's blog content. My passion for creative writing and extensive experience in the content industry makes me confident that I am the ideal candidate for this role.

In my previous roles, I have consistently delivered high-quality work and received positive feedback from colleagues and clients. I am confident I can bring the same dedication and professionalism to your organization and contribute to its success.

"If we have the attitude that it's going to be a great day, it usually is."

J 2 Why Do You Want To Leave (Or Have Left) Your Job?

Give an honest and positive answer to why you left your previous job, and it is important to be direct and stick to the facts while also focusing on the future. Even if you quit under challenging circumstances, it is not the best time to share too much information with the interviewer. Instead, showing interest in the new position you are applying for and explaining how it will afford you career growth and development is important.

Some of the reasons that you can give for leaving your previous job include a desire to take on less responsibility, wanting to relocate, a desire for a career change, a desire for career growth and development, a desire to improve work/life balance, a wish to learn new skills, a longing to take on more responsibility, no longer being interested in the company's vision and goals, or a desire for a shorter commute to work.

It is important to remember that speaking poorly of your previous boss during an interview may reflect poorly on you and give the potential employer reason to doubt your loyalty and professionalism. By focusing on your positive reasons for wanting to take up the new role, you can frame your answer in a way that casts you in a positive light and highlights your interest in the new position.

Sample 1

In my current role, I have managed a team of 15 individuals. Through this experience, I have developed essential skills such as resource management and client servicing. Additionally, I have had the pleasure of leading my team to surpass our projected targets for the last three quarters.

While I have greatly enjoyed my time with my current organization, I am eager to take on a larger team and expand my responsibilities. Though my current employer has offered me a promotion, this opening with your organization is the logical next step in my career growth.

I am drawn to your organization because of its reputation for fostering a culture of growth and development. I believe that working with your team will enable me to continue to challenge myself professionally and take my skills to the next level. I am excited about the potential to lead a larger team, tackle more complex projects, and make a meaningful impact within your organization.

Sample 2

I am lucky to have landed a job at ABC Company fresh out of college. I have learned a lot about digital marketing there, and working alongside the creative team has been a stimulating experience. However, I feel it is time to take the next step in my career. I have always been a natural leader and am ready to move into a management position. Unfortunately, ABC Company already has highly skilled and competent managers in place who are not likely to leave anytime soon.

Nevertheless, I have taken advantage of supplementary management training courses while working at ABC Company, which have prepared me for the responsibilities and challenges of a managerial role. I am confident that my experience and knowledge will allow me to hit the ground running as the next digital marketing manager in your company. I am eager to apply my skills, take on new challenges, and help drive your business forward.

Sample 3

My reason for the job change is the termination of my contract. For the past two years, I have worked on a contractual basis as a contractor at several locations, spending 90% of my time traveling from one city/country to another.

I needed a stationary full-time job with minimal travel to develop my project management skills and explore other fields.

I was captivated when I read the advertisement for this particular job opening! Working under stellar leadership and honing my skills is a good opportunity. I am passionate about such a work environment and have the same views as your organization on zero waste and inclusive growth.

Interestingly, I reduced wastage in my department by 37% at my current organization by suggesting that we only generate e-bills! I am sure that with my diverse background, I will be of great service to this firm.

Sample 4

Our biggest clients were leaving the market, forcing my company to dissolve some positions. Unfortunately, my position was one of the newest positions created in the department at that time, and it was disbanded.

I am pleased about my stay in my previous employment because I did learn a lot that will help me propel my career to the next level.

Sample 5

My current employer is going through corporate optimization, and my department will be laid off. The reason for the job change is that the higher management told me to look for other avenues of work, and they have accommodated me during this transition period of 90 days.

I have a strong technical foundation and constantly update my skills through online courses and timely certifications. I want to diversify my profile and work with a larger client base. My current employer works with only 11 clients, and I know your company caters to over 50+ clients.

This presents a challenging and exciting prospect for me. I am keen to utilize my potential and skills to add value to your company.

Sample 6

The management of my previous organization experienced a reformation, and I was assigned a new line manager.

Working with the new manager, it became apparent that my new manager had expectations that did not match my strengths.

After a while, my manager recommended that he bring in someone he had worked with who had a better experience in the local and international markets, and I was replaced.

I learned that my most vital strengths were customer service rather than project management. I know that my customer service skills will be a great asset to a role like this that focuses on improving customer experience.

Sample 7

I am seeking a job change because I am looking for upward mobility and financial growth in my career. I have had the privilege of working with my current employer for the past four years, during which time I have had the opportunity to learn and grow significantly. I am grateful for the experience, which instilled a spectacular work ethic and deep industry knowledge.

However, I have realized that my work is no longer challenging. I have exhausted all avenues for growth within the organization and am looking for a new opportunity to continue progressing in my career.

I am excited about the prospect of interacting and working closely with the thought leaders of our industry who are part of the leadership team at your organization. Being part of a dynamic and forward-thinking team will allow me to continue to learn and grow in my profession. I am eager to contribute my skills and expertise to help the organization achieve its goals and objectives.

I am committed to pursuing excellence in all aspects of my work. I am confident that my dedication, experience, and skills will make me a valuable addition to your team.

Sample 8

My job change is because I was terminated from my previous job due to a misunderstanding resulting from poor communication skills. At the time, I misunderstood my supervisor's instructions and ended up setting a higher monthly spend on an ad account for a client. This led to a loss of a few hundred dollars, which, in retrospect, was not significant. However, the relationship with the client was already strained, and this incident caused them to leave.

The experience was a turning point for me, and I took it as an opportunity to improve my communication skills. I realized that clear and effective communication is critical in any work environment and that misunderstandings can lead to serious consequences.

Since then, I have worked very hard to enhance my verbal and written communication skills, and I have taken various training programs and workshops to develop these essential skills. I have also learned to be more attentive to instructions and clarify them before taking action.

I believe that this experience has helped me to become a better professional and has instilled in me a deep sense of accountability and responsibility. I am confident that my improved communication skills will be an asset in my future roles, and I am excited to apply my knowledge and expertise to contribute to my new team's success.

"Success is no accident. It is hard work, perseverance, learning, studying, sacrifice, and most of all, love of what you are doing or learning to do."

K 1 How Do You Evaluate Success?

When asked, How do you define success? , during a job interview, it is important to understand that the employer seeks more than just a generic answer. They want to know about your work ethic, goals, personality, and what drives you to succeed.

To impress the hiring manager, showcasing your determination, motivation, drive, enthusiasm, and ability to work collaboratively toward a shared vision is essential. You can do this by providing specific examples of your successes in the past and explaining the factors that contributed to your achievements.

For instance, you can talk about how you were a quality-conscious and improvement-oriented employee in your previous job. You can mention a particular project or task that you worked on and describe how you went above and beyond to ensure its success. You can also highlight how you collaborated with your team members to achieve a common goal.

It is important to emphasize the skills and traits that make you an asset to the company. For example, if you are applying for a sales position, you could talk about how you exceeded your sales targets in your previous role by building strong relationships with your clients and going the extra mile to meet their needs.

Answering the question, How do you define success? , is an opportunity to showcase your strengths and demonstrate why you are the right candidate for the job.

Sample 1

I define success in multiple ways. At work, success means meeting the goals and expectations set by my supervisors and collaborating with my co-workers to achieve a common objective. After all, I believe teamwork is essential to achieving success in any work environment.

In researching your company, I was impressed to learn that it has a reputation for recognizing and rewarding success. I am also interested in the opportunities for growth and advancement available to employees here. I believe that this aligns with my definition of success and is one of the reasons I am excited about this job opportunity.

Outside of work, I enjoy playing softball. Success on the field is more than just winning the game. It's about teamwork, communication, and pushing myself to improve. I always seek ways to enhance my skills and support my teammates.

Sample 2

Success means achieving the company's goals and the client's satisfaction. During my last position, I found it most fulfilling when I assisted clients in finding the ideal solution to their problems. My supervisors frequently recognized my aptitude for effectively communicating and empathizing with my coworkers and customers. I am convinced these skills will transfer well to this new role and align with this company's philosophy of success.

In my opinion, a significant aspect of success is collaboration. The ability to work effectively with others towards a common objective is critical. I appreciate that your company values a team-oriented approach to success and prioritizes creating a positive work environment that nurtures this approach. I am excited about possibly joining a company that encourages a sense of shared purpose and values its employees.

Sample 3

I firmly believe that individual accomplishments do not solely determine personal success but the entire team's success. In my opinion, a successful team is one where each member works collaboratively to achieve common goals. As a member of the accounting department, I have always strived to ensure that my work complements and supports that of my colleagues. I understand that my numbers and calculations are only as good as the accuracy of the information I receive from my coworkers and vice versa.

I have communicated and collaborated with my colleagues throughout my career to ensure our team succeeds. For instance, in my previous role, I was part of a team that successfully reduced the turnaround time for processing invoices by 30%. This was achieved by implementing a new invoicing system, which I suggested after consulting with my colleagues.

I believe this company values a strong work ethic and a community spirit, and I am confident that my collaborative mindset and dedication to achieving common goals will be a great asset to the team. I am excited about the opportunity to work alongside like-minded individuals to drive the company's success.

Sample 4

Your statement about success resonates with me as I believe in positively impacting other people's lives. I find fulfillment in my work when I can help someone solve a problem, overcome a challenge, or achieve a goal. In my previous role, I worked in the healthcare industry, and success meant improving my patients' health and well-being. I took pride in providing them with personalized care, and it was rewarding to see them leave the hospital feeling better than when they arrived.

I am excited about the opportunity to work for a company like yours, known for its dedication to making a difference in the community. From what I have read and heard about your company, you strongly focus on corporate social responsibility and giving back to society. I am eager to participate in that effort and contribute my skills and experience to further that mission.

Sample 5

As a team player, I believe that success is not just about individual accomplishments but also about the collective achievements of the team. I strive to work collaboratively with my colleagues to achieve our common goals and objectives. Success means meeting our targets and completing projects within the allocated timelines and budgets.

As a team leader in my previous position, I made sure that I set clear expectations and goals for my team. I encouraged my team members to share their ideas and insights, and we worked together to develop a plan to achieve our objectives. I also made sure to recognize and acknowledge the contributions of each team member, as I firmly believe that everyone's effort is essential to the team's success.

When evaluating success, I look at the bigger picture and assess the results and the process. I believe in continuous improvement and always seek feedback to understand how to improve my performance and contribute more effectively to the team's success. Ultimately, I define success as a combination of individual and collective accomplishments where everyone on the team feels valued and fulfilled.

Sample 6

There is no greater feeling of accomplishment than seeing a project through to completion, especially when challenging. I firmly believe that success can only be achieved when everyone on the team works towards a common goal. In my previous position, I was part of a team responsible for developing a new product line for our company. We faced many challenges, but with everyone working together and utilizing their unique skills and strengths, we could meet our established deadlines and quality standards.

Through this experience, I learned that communication and collaboration are key to achieving success in a team project. I kept the lines of communication open and actively sought input and feedback from my team members. I also made a point to recognize and appreciate their contributions, which helped to boost morale and motivation.

I believe that success is not just about meeting individual goals but rather about working together as a team to accomplish a shared objective.

Sample 7

As a manager, achieving outstanding metrics and quantifying achievements is my top priority. However, I also believe success is more than hitting targets and reaching goals. It's about fostering a positive work environment and motivating my team to do their best work.

In the past, I have found success by setting realistic goals for my team and celebrating when we met or exceeded them. I make it a point to regularly praise my team for their hard work and dedication, which boosts morale and helps build a strong team dynamic.

I believe aligning my definition of success with my employer is crucial in achieving a productive and successful working relationship. By understanding and working towards the company's goals and values, I am confident that I can contribute to the company's and my team's growth and success.

"Every successful person in the world is a hustler in one way or another. We all hustle to get where we need to be. Only a fool would sit around and wait on another man to feed him."

K 2 Do You Consider Yourself Successful?

Reflecting on past achievements is crucial in identifying strengths and areas of expertise. It's important to remember that success is relative, and what may be considered a significant achievement to one person may not be the same for another. It's all about understanding your goals and values and how they align with the company's mission and vision.

When discussing past achievements in an interview, it's essential to focus on your impact on the team or organization. For instance, you could talk about a time when you successfully led a team through a challenging project, overcame obstacles to achieve a goal, or effectively managed your time to complete a project on time and within budget.

Providing specific examples of how you achieved success is essential. For example, if you exceeded sales targets, you could explain the specific strategies you employed to achieve those results. This would demonstrate your determination, work ethic, and ability to adapt and solve problems.

In addition to discussing past successes, it's also essential to highlight future goals and aspirations. This demonstrates that you have a growth mindset and always seek new challenges and opportunities to improve. For example, you could discuss how you hope to continue building on your success in sales by learning new sales techniques or exploring new markets.

In summary, when discussing past achievements in an interview, it's crucial to focus on the impact you had on the team or organization, provide specific examples of how you achieved success, and highlight future goals and aspirations to demonstrate your growth mind.

Sample 1

I may not have a long list of impressive accomplishments, but I believe my personal growth and resilience in adversity make me successful. When my parents passed away, I had to learn how to support myself at a young age. It was a difficult time, but it taught me the importance of independence and responsibility. I also had to deal with various health issues that made it hard to keep up with my studies. But I refused to let that hold me back, and I worked hard to take care of myself, changing my habits and lifestyle to become healthier.

Despite the challenges, I graduated from high school and earned my certification. I'm proud of myself for not giving up and for the hard work and determination it took to get here. Success is not just about external achievements but also about overcoming obstacles and becoming a better person because of them.

My life experiences have given me a unique perspective and a strong empathy for others who may be struggling. I am committed to working hard and using my skills and abilities to make a positive impact in whatever role I take on.

Sample 2

In addition to my project management success, I am proud of my ability to learn quickly and adapt to new situations. In my previous role, I was asked to take on a new client account with a complex set of requirements I had never encountered before. Rather than feeling overwhelmed, I researched the client's needs and worked with my team to develop a creative solution that exceeded their expectations. This not only earned us the client's trust and long-term business but also earned me recognition from my superiors.

I believe that success is not just about achieving individual goals but also about being a team player and contributing to the success of others. For instance, I actively sought opportunities to mentor and train new hires in my department. As a result, several of them have achieved great success in their roles, and I am proud to have played a small part in their development.

Finally, I think having a positive attitude and a growth mindset is essential to achieve success. I approach every challenge as an opportunity to learn and grow and always look for ways to improve my skills and knowledge. My positive attitude and determination to succeed make me a valuable asset to any team.

Sample 3

In addition to my ability to get along well with others, I am also proud of my problem-solving skills. In my previous role, I was tasked with finding a solution to a recurring problem plaguing the company for months. I approached the situation systematically, gathering information, analyzing data, and brainstorming potential solutions with my team. Eventually, we found a solution that solved the problem and saved the company a significant amount of money.

I am constantly looking for ways to improve myself and my skills. I make sure to keep up with industry trends and attend relevant training sessions and conferences to stay up to date. Continuous learning is crucial for personal and professional growth and essential to my definition of success.

Outside of work, I am also involved in my community, volunteering for local charities and organizations. Giving back to others and positively impacting my community is another source of success and fulfillment.

Success is about achieving individual goals and positively impacting those around me, whether my colleagues, clients, or community. I am confident that my skills, personality, and values align with your company's vision of success, and I look forward to the opportunity to contribute to your team.

Sample 4

I believe that success is a continuous journey, and I feel like I have achieved a lot so far, but I also know that there is always more room for growth and improvement. As a son, I have always tried to be there for my family and support them in any way I can, and as a father, I strive to be a positive role model for my children and provide for them.

In my professional life, I have succeeded as a salesman and consistently achieved good numbers throughout my career. However, I am not satisfied with just maintaining the status quo. I have a burning desire to continue to grow and excel in my career. I always seek new challenges and opportunities to improve my skills and abilities.

One thing that has helped me achieve success is my competitiveness. Healthy competition is essential in driving oneself to reach their full potential. I have always enjoyed the thrill of a good challenge and the satisfaction of achieving my goals.

While I am proud of my past successes, I am not complacent. I always seek ways to improve and reach new heights personally and professionally. I believe that this drive and determination are what sets me apart and make me successful,

Sample 5

Success is not just about achieving specific goals or receiving recognition for my work. It is more about the satisfaction and sense of fulfillment that comes from knowing that my work is meaningful and impactful. True success at work means adding value to the company and its customers and positively contributing to the world.

To achieve this success, I focus on excelling in my performance and continually learning and growing in my role. I take on key job assignments and challenges as opportunities to develop new skills and knowledge, and I always strive to exceed expectations.

One of the key indicators of success for me is the sense of fulfillment that comes from seeing the results of my work. I want to know that my efforts have made a difference, whether in improving efficiency, delivering high-quality products or services, or creating a better customer experience. Success is about finding fulfillment and meaning in my work and positively impacting the world around me.

Sample 6

To me, success means more than just achieving a high salary or a prestigious title. Instead, I find fulfillment in spending most of my time focused on work that is meaningful to me and helps contribute to the growth and success of the organization I work for.

As I strive for success, I continually increase my efficiency and productivity. By doing so, I can become a more valuable asset to my organization and ultimately help to drive its growth and success.

However, I recognize that individual success can only take an organization so far. I firmly believe working as a team towards a common goal can achieve the greatest success. Collaboration and teamwork are essential to achieving long-term success, as they allow us to combine our strengths and skills to achieve more than we could individually. Success combines personal fulfillment, increasing efficiency to contribute to the organization's growth, and working collaboratively with others toward a common goal.

Sample 7

Yes, goal-setting has been essential to my career journey thus far. Throughout my career, which spans several years, I have learned the importance of setting clear, achievable goals for myself and ensuring that I work towards meeting each of them.

I have also learned to be resilient in facing obstacles to reach my goals. Instead of letting challenges and setbacks discourage me, I use them as opportunities to learn and grow. I believe every obstacle can be overcome with perseverance and determination, and I am always willing to put in the extra effort needed to achieve my goals.

As I consider the new position I am applying for, I am excited about its potential to take my career to the next level. This unique opportunity will enable me to set even higher goals for myself and work towards achieving them in a more challenging and rewarding environment.

I am confident that my experience and skills make me a strong candidate for this new role. I am excited to contribute to the organization's success and continue to grow and develop professionally. I look forward to demonstrating my abilities and taking on new challenges in this exciting new role.

"Hustle in silence and let your success make the noise."

L 1 What Are You Passionate About?

Passion refers to those areas, topics, or activities that ignite enthusiasm and curiosity. They are the things that make you feel alive and engaged in life, and they can vary widely from person to person. A passion can be anything from a hobby or sport to a subject of study or a cause you care deeply about.

What sets passions apart from other interests is the intensity of feeling that they evoke. When you are passionate about something, it energizes and motivates you to pursue it with vigor and dedication. Your passion can give you a sense of purpose and direction and help you find meaning and fulfillment in your life.

Although passions don't have to be related to work, they can be. Having a job that aligns with your desires can make work feel less like a chore and more fulfilling. You may feel more engaged, motivated, and productive when doing something you love. On the other hand, if you don't have the opportunity to pursue your passions at work, it can lead to boredom, disengagement, and frustration.

Passions are vital to our identity and can enrich our lives in countless ways. Whether through creative, intellectual, or physical pursuit, following our passions can help us cultivate a sense of purpose and joy that can last a lifetime.

It drives you to stay focused and disciplined personally and professionally. It also highlights how your dedication to the sport has helped you develop time management skills, which are valuable in any workplace. This demonstrates your ability to balance multiple commitments and use your passions to motivate you to achieve your goals on and off the court.

Sample 1

Tennis is a big part of my life and something I'm passionate about. In my spare time, I train regularly and even compete as a semi-professional player. I've dedicated a lot of time to this sport, and my vacation time in the past few years has been spent traveling around the country to participate in competitions. Playing tennis has given me the drive and focus to be productive at work and helps me manage my time more efficiently. By staying organized and disciplined, I can complete my tasks efficiently and still have time for training.

Sample 2

Maintaining good health is my top priority, and I'm passionate about fitness. I make it a point to work out four or five times a week and keep a daily journal of my meals. This approach has helped me stay disciplined, understand what works for me, and identify areas where I can improve. I also use my journal to track my short- and long-term fitness goals, which helps me stay motivated and focused.

Sample 3

Healthy living and healthy eating are things that I'm passionate about. My parents instilled these values in me from a young age, and I've carried them throughout my life. That's why I enjoy working in the fitness industry so much. It's a career that allows me to blend my interests and passions with my professional life. I feel like I'm working on something important and meaningful, which motivates me to do my best work and help people reach their fitness goals.

Sample 4

My biggest passion is learning about software and technology. Computers have fascinated me from a young age, so I pursued a degree in Computer Science in college. Since then, I have continued exploring this field, which has been an excellent choice. As a front-end software developer, I get to shape the direction of the internet and the evolution of websites. This is an exciting opportunity for me, and it's fulfilling to see my work make a difference in how people interact with digital technology.

Sample 5

I'm passionate about hiking and being outdoors. Something about being out in nature rejuvenates me and gives me a sense of peace and clarity. That's how I usually spend my weekends and free time when I'm not in the office. When I hike or spend time outside, I have more energy and focus when I return to work on Mondays. The fresh air and exercise help me recharge and approach my work with renewed enthusiasm.

Sample 6

Unfortunately, I lost my father to pancreatic cancer, which was a life-changing event for me. Since then, I've been passionate about raising awareness and funds for cancer research. I volunteer for CRY, an advocacy group, and am part of their volunteer network. Through my work with CRY, I have been able to contribute to the fight against cancer in various ways, from organizing fundraising events to advocating for policy changes that can make a difference. One of the things that I find most rewarding about volunteering is getting to know patients and survivors personally. Hearing their stories and seeing their strength and resilience in the face of this disease is truly inspiring, and it motivates me to do more to help find a cure.

Sample 7

One area that I'm particularly passionate about is self-development and self-improvement. Investing in yourself and continually learning is essential for personal growth and success. In terms of my professional life, my passion for self-development has led me to pursue customer service roles. Through my work, I have gained valuable communication, listening, and problem-solving skills that have helped me excel in my job and personal life. I have more confidence in my interactions with others and am better equipped to handle difficult situations at work and in my relationships. Additionally, my passion for learning has led me to take on new challenges and learn new things, which has been incredibly rewarding. Overall, I believe that investing in self-development is essential for personal and professional growth, and it's something that I'm genuinely passionate about.

Sample 8

I am deeply passionate about painting. It's something that I look forward to every week and find highly fulfilling. It is a way for me to unwind and de-stress after a busy week, and it also helps me be more creative in other areas of my life. As an artist, I'm constantly seeking new ways to express myself and interpret the world around me. This same mindset carries over into my work life, where I always look for creative solutions to problems. My passion for painting has helped me be more open-minded and think outside the box when tackling challenges in my job. Some of my most creative ideas and solutions have come to me while I'm painting in the studio. Overall, I find that painting is a gratifying hobby that not only brings me joy but also helps me to be more creative and innovative in all aspects of my life.

Sample 9

I am very passionate about baking. The entire process gratifies me, from researching new recipes to testing them out. I've been documenting my baking experiences for three years and even started my blog. Baking allows me to be very detail-oriented, and I love the scientific aspects of it, such as measuring ingredients and adjusting recipes to achieve the perfect result.

One of the things I love most about baking is that it also allows me to be social. I often use my baking as an excuse to get together with friends and family, and I love the sense of community that comes with sharing my creations. Every year around the holiday season, I host a massive cookie swap with friends, which is always fun.

Having a passion outside of work is important, as it helps balance my life and keeps me energized and motivated. And while baking may not be directly related to my career, the skills, and qualities I develop through it, such as attention to detail and creativity, have proven valuable assets in my professional life.

"Every champion was once a contender that did not give up."

L 2 How Do You Describe Your Leadership Style?

They can inquire directly about what leadership means to you, whether you consider yourself a leader or a follower. I would describe my leadership style as result-oriented. In an ideal case, I'd like to have goals in place for every single employee, regardless of how simple their job is.

Once we have the goals in place, we can set milestones or daily schedules for everyone, and I can lead them on their way to continuously attain their goals by checking their progress daily, making sure they know what they are supposed to do, delegating work, counseling them, and so on. I also need to lead people so they can see the bigger picture. That's why I make it a point to personally explain to everyone the role their work plays on the final product and their role in the team. In my experience, it works wonders with their motivation.

Sample 1

Leadership is about creating a positive work environment where everyone feels valued and can contribute ideas. As a democratic leader, I encourage open communication and actively seek input from my team members. We can develop the best possible solutions by involving everyone in decision-making.

I also believe in creating a culture of collaboration and teamwork. I lead by example and am always willing to roll up my sleeves and work alongside my team members to achieve our goals. I understand that everyone has their strengths and weaknesses, and I strive to create an environment where we can all support each other and work towards a common goal.

Another important aspect of my leadership style is empowerment. I believe that by empowering my team members to take ownership of their work and make decisions independently, I can help them grow professionally and personally. This also helps build trust and respect within the team, which is essential for success.

My goal as a leader is to create a positive and productive work environment where everyone feels valued and motivated to do their best work. I believe we can achieve great things together by empowering my team members, encouraging collaboration, and leading by example.

Sample 2

As an affinitive leader, I prioritize building strong relationships with my team members. I believe that creating a positive and supportive work environment helps to increase productivity and employee morale. In addition to considering how decisions may affect my team members, I encourage open communication and feedback. By fostering an environment where employees feel comfortable expressing their opinions, we can work together to achieve our goals and overcome challenges.

In my previous role as a scheduling manager, I took into account the personal circumstances of my team members when creating the work schedule. For example, I noticed that some of our employees were single mothers, and I recognized that scheduling them for night shifts may not be the best option for their situation. I created a more supportive work environment and built stronger relationships with my team members by being sensitive to their needs.

My leadership style is focused on creating a positive and supportive work environment where team members feel valued and supported. I believe that by prioritizing the needs of my team members, we can work together to achieve our goals and create a successful organization.

Sample 3

As a leader of a team of seven creative individuals in the graphic design department, I found that the most effective way to lead was by setting an overall direction for the team and communicating the final goals for each campaign. I firmly believe that providing a clear and concise vision is essential in ensuring everyone is aligned and working towards the same objectives.

At the same time, I also understood the importance of giving my team members the freedom to brainstorm, dream, and imagine their ideas and to work independently to achieve their goals. In my experience, this has led to higher creativity and innovation, as each team member can contribute their unique perspective and ideas.

It is essential to have regular team meetings to ensure that everyone is on track and progressing toward their goals. During these meetings, I would offer feedback and encouragement to help my team members stay motivated and focused. My leadership style allows for a healthy balance of direction and independence, ultimately leading to a more productive and creative team. I would love to bring this approach to your company and lead your team to success.

Sample 4

Your leadership style of being results-oriented and setting goals for each employee is great for ensuring that everyone is focused and productive. It's also commendable that you take the time to explain to your team members the bigger picture of their work and how it contributes to the final product. This helps them to see the value in what they are doing and how it fits into the larger goals of the team and the company. I think it's important also to acknowledge the individual strengths and weaknesses of each team member and to provide them with the necessary support and resources to help them achieve their goals. This could include mentoring, training, or providing a supportive environment where they can feel comfortable asking questions or seeking feedback.

Another aspect of being results-oriented is holding people accountable for their work. While being supportive, setting expectations and holding people to them is also important. This could include regular check-ins, performance reviews, or regular feedback sessions. By doing this, you can ensure that everyone meets their goals and contributes to the team's success.

Sample 5

I would describe myself as a flexible leader. In my long managerial career, I've led various people and teams and learned that different things work with other people and groups. Hence, I do not limit myself to only one leadership style. Adapting to different situations and team dynamics is a key trait of a good leader.

As a leader, I prioritize assessing my team member's strengths and weaknesses. This allows me to assign tasks that fit their skills well and provide feedback and training in areas where they need improvement. Additionally, I like to test their decision-making ability with seemingly trivial decisions to see how they handle them. If I see that the team works great without decisive intervention from my side, I won't intervene. Still, if the motivation drops quickly or other problems occur in the team, such as regular conflicts, I will opt for a more authoritative leadership style.

I also believe that exceptional individuals require special attention, especially those who show potential to be leaders. In such cases, I prefer to work with them as a coach, providing guidance and mentorship as they navigate their professional development.

My leadership style is all about adaptability and situational awareness. I try to adjust my approach to the people I lead, the situation in the business, and other circumstances, while keeping the business's long-term goals in mind. By doing so, I believe I can achieve the best results for the company and create a positive work environment for my team.

Sample 6

I understand your perspective on the importance of being a strict authoritative leader in a construction environment. However, I would like to offer some insights into the different leadership styles that may be effective in this setting.

A transformational leadership style could inspire and motivate workers to strive for excellence. By providing them with a sense of purpose and meaning behind their work, they may become more invested in their job and more willing to put in extra effort. Similarly, a servant leadership style could also be effective in the construction industry. By putting the needs of the workers first and creating a supportive work environment, you can foster a sense of trust and loyalty among the team. This, in turn, could lead to higher productivity and job satisfaction.

I understand the importance of setting specific goals and deadlines to ensure the work is completed efficiently and on time. However, involving the workers in this process may also be beneficial by setting achievable goals together. This can increase their sense of ownership and commitment to the project.

While a strict authoritative leadership style may be effective in certain situations, it's important to be open to different leadership styles that may also be effective in a construction environment.

Sample 7

This is my first application for a leadership job, and it is hard to define my leadership style at work. However, I have experience leading some sports teams, such as at college or with friends. And I would characterize myself as a positive leader.

I never hesitate to recognize someone for a good job, praising them for their work. In my opinion, praise beats criticism. I also **try to lead by example.** I would never ask someone to stay longer at work if I was to leave on time. I believe this approach can yield great results, though I haven't tested it in a corporate environment yet.

Sample 8

Yes, I agree that it's crucial to maintain a balance between independence and intervention as a leader. Allowing team members to work independently can foster creativity and ownership of their work, but it's also important to step in when needed to provide guidance, feedback, and motivation.

Another aspect of effective leadership that I believe is important is communication. As a leader, I strive to communicate clearly and effectively with my team members, ensuring everyone is on the same page and understands the goals and expectations. I also encourage open communication within the team, where team members can share their ideas, feedback, and concerns with me.

I believe that a good leader should lead by example. I try to demonstrate the qualities and behaviors I expect from my team members, such as professionalism, honesty, hard work, and a positive attitude. By setting a good example, I hope to inspire my team members to follow suit and strive for excellence in their work.

"You've got to get up every morning with determination if you're going to go to bed with satisfaction."

M 1 Where Do You See Yourself In 5 Years?

Employers ask this question for two reasons:

The employer wants to know how long you plan to stay in the position.

The employer wants to know if your vision aligns with the company's.

It would help you never to forget that a recruiter's job is to get the right candidate to stay and grow in the organization. They want to know your career goals, satisfaction with the position, and how hard and long you are willing to grow and stay in the company.

Sample 1

In 5 years, I would love to complete my internal and external training program for my position. I have read about it on your website, and I think it is an amazing opportunity for me to learn. I don't only look forward to getting the right training for my role, but it will quicken my journey to becoming a marketing manager, which is my career goal. My ideal track would be creating awareness in rural areas. I learned that getting your product to rural places is one goal this company wants to achieve.

Sample 2

When asked where I see myself five years from now, I never figured out how to respond. Then I realized that the answer was in front of me. I was never decisive enough so that people could rely on me. I want to continue working on this part. In the five years, I see myself making calculated decisions for my professional career growth. Earning reliability is my primary objective. I want the administration to lay their trust in me. This can help me to give positive results. Earning credibility can lead me to new responsibilities. Performing those with great zeal can improve credibility to a new level. This correlated cycle is advantageous to any individual. In five years, I hope I hit the target I have aimed for.

Sample 3

I want to become a Senior Business Consultant within the next five years. During this period, I would like to accomplish the following:

Help organization improve their business

Create a personal network of highly specialized professionals

Learn as much as I can about optimizing and improving clients' businesses, as well as the essentials of operating a company

Sample 4

I aim to find a career spot that ensures continued growth alongside daily new challenges.

Three years from now, I see myself as an experienced and reliable team senior; five years from now, I assume I will be ready to take up managerial responsibilities like product strategy.

I want a stable career in a single organization and hope to get the same wherever I start.

Sample 5

Well, I'm excited about this opening. I want to be recognized as an industry expert in five years. This job will give me a golden opportunity to do the same. Since I already have a few years of work experience, I am excited to take up managerial responsibilities in the coming years.

Besides, I have the potential to lead projects, and if I can deliver, I am sure this organization will give me the chance to become one of the forerunners. I want to mention that in the past, I have worked with some fantastic managers. Under them, I have become a professional with excellent managerial skills. Five years ago, I wanted to be where I am today. So five years from now, I want to set realistic goals for myself and my organization. I will keep the same fire alive and hope to achieve my goal.

Sample 6

Judging by my previous assumptions, I have seldom landed where I wanted to. It can be due to the unclear goals I have set. Due to the very same reason, I started setting up smaller targets, which led me to this place. Keeping this habit intact, I want to add some bigger targets. I want to work with your organization, doing my best for my assigned tasks. During these years, I want to perform what is expected of me. If required, I will consider myself responsible for leading the team which can provide desired outcomes to this reputed organization. It is not as easy as it seems. I hope my decisions are rewarding in the end.

Sample 7

I'm excited to be handling the marketing side of a few products in your company. In a few years, I would like to see myself heading the marketing campaigns of not just one product but many diverse products in your company, increasing the outreach of the products. I would love to expand to other verticals and see myself being an expert in product marketing and brand management.

Sample 8

I am propelled to be the best at what I do, and I want to work in an organization that will allow me to develop my skills, handle interesting projects, and be part of a team I can learn from. Many creative thinkers in the industry work here, so I would love to build a career here.

Sample 9

Let me mention that I have never been filled with such enthusiasm for any job position ever before. It is because this job is what I have always desired. I assure you that I am not polishing my words according to desperation. I had set up my career goals to reach this point. Having done that, I look forward to giving my best in every aspect. The experience I have gathered in my career can be helpful for this job position. Also, I can help recruits to settle down well within the working environment. I can guide them further to the point where they can elaborate their ideas for the progress of this organization. For me, this is an objective that is worth working for. In five years, I see myself sharing the experience with the team for the benefit of all.

Sample 10

I have always set my priorities in life. Today I can say that those priorities have helped me achieve various things. Those decisions have allowed me to sit in a reputed organization. It is almost certain that I have set up priorities for the upcoming years. I look forward to working here with a promising attitude. I want to attain new heights in my career while taking on the goal of this organization. I must synchronize my targets with the objectives of this company. Then it can be easier for me to work to my full potential. The five years ahead can be marked with progress milestones for me and the organization.

"No one is to blame for your future situation but yourself."

M 2 What Do You Like Least About Your Job?

This question can seem like a net to trap you because the recruiter looks forward to getting a negative response from you. So if you give the interviewer the impression that you were dissatisfied with your previous job, the interviewer may have the impression that you may also be dissatisfied with the position you applied for.

Avoid talking about personal issues you have with co-workers in the office. Avoid answers that will make you appear as a persistent person. Avoid giving the interviewer the impression that you are difficult to please. Don't use this question as an opportunity to start bad-mouthing your previous boss or company.

Sample 1

I liked my previous employer and the talented people on my team. One of the challenges I faced was working remotely from my location, which became more challenging as the company grew. I was also tired of limiting myself to working alone. I am enthusiastic about this job because it will allow me to work remotely when needed.

I look forward to connecting with team members physically and not online.

Sample 2

I really cannot say I dislike anything about my current job. My company is a start-up that is still in its infancy stage, which gives little room for advancement. I think I have reached the peak of my career in my current organization. I want to learn more about technology because the world is becoming technologically based. Regrettably, we don't work with technology-based tools. To advance my career, I've decided it is time to move on.

Sample 3

It is a great company, but my position kept me behind the scenes (I was always in the computer room), with very little interaction with co-workers and customers. I love solving computer or gadget-related problems, but I value human relations a lot too. This is why I am enthusiastic about this job.

When answering this question, be careful not to go negative about your current job and employer. The easiest way to handle this question with poise is to focus on an opportunity for the role you're interviewing for offers that your current job doesn't. You can keep the conversation positive and emphasize your excitement about the job. By concentrating on the positives of the new employer, you can avoid mentioning anything explicitly negative about your current job.

Sample 4

While I enjoyed working for a large law firm because I gained experience across several subject matters, I'd prefer to bring all those learning to your firm because I believe that your singular focus on the entertainment industry would allow me to have a more profound impact.

This answer briefly mentions a current responsibility but focuses on the opportunity the new job would provide.

Sample 5

In my current role, I'm responsible for pitching media lists. While I've developed a knack for this and can do it when necessary, I'm looking forward to a job with a more hands-on role in working with media partners. That is one of the things that most excited me about your Account Supervisor position.

There is always the bold option: to speak more bluntly and directly about something not-so-great about your current role or company. But again, you'll want to end on a positive note that spotlights your enthusiasm for the new job.

Sample 6

My current company acquires new business through traditional methods like cold calling and direct mail. I'm impressed with the digital, email, and social acquisition campaigns you have implemented and how they reflect a more modern, innovative approach. While I am flexible enough to succeed in diverse work environments, I'm eager to work for a company that embraces change.

Sample 7

The company was growing quickly, so it was a bit disorganized, and I often had multiple supervisors and senior team members giving me different instructions. However, this was an excellent opportunity to improve my ability to work under pressure and communication skills. For example, I had to learn to communicate clearly and quickly to clarify with my managers and team if there was a conflict in what I had been asked to do. I enjoyed most aspects of the job and liked working in such a fast-paced environment. It just took some adjustment. It was a great learning experience for me.

Sample 8

What I like least about my job right now is the limited opportunities to advance and be promoted in the company. It's a great organization, and

I've learned a lot here, but it's such a small company that finding ways to move up is challenging unless somebody retires or leaves. My group is only four people, for example. That's one reason I'm job searching right now; I'm looking for a larger organization that can offer more opportunities in the long term for upward movement and career progression.

"Getting over a painful experience is much like crossing the monkey bars. You must let go at some point to move forward."

N 1 What is the Difference Between Hard Work and Smart Work?

The difference between smart and hard work is based on how you approach the task. Hard work means spending long hours to complete the job without any shortcuts. It gives us the desired results, but the process is long and stressful. In contrast, smart work will provide the same result by planning and prioritization tasks.

Sample 1

Hard work is like trying to push a big rock downhill with your bare hands, and smart work would be using a lever to push down the same rock!

I think smart work and hard work go hand in hand. At the beginning of my career, I was a classic hard worker. I took instructions, understood my job, and would immediately start working towards completing the task. Over the last five years, I have observed seniors and equipped myself with crucial skills.

Today I can do a mundane job in less time than I used to. For instance, I use popular browser plugins allowed by my office to detect plagiarism, eliminate grammar errors and improve any text in emails and documents. I also use online spell-checker tools to double-check my drafts. I feel I have developed as a smart worker.

But I firmly believe no one can be a smart worker without working hard first.

Sample 2

The difference between hard work and smart work is based on how I approach my task. Hard work would mean spending long hours completing my work without shortcuts. It ensures results, but the process is long and stressful. Smart work would aim for the same results but with planning and prioritization of tasks.

In Law College, the trend of examination questions was repetitive. The questions asked in the last few years would be asked again. I realized this after my first semester. Since then, I would only study the previous five years' exam questions. I would focus on studying everything else for the rest of the year.

Therefore I worked hard to study the entire syllabus for my knowledge and worked smartly to score well in my examinations. A combination of both has guaranteed me the best possible results always!

Sample 3

A smart worker sets goals and is constantly working towards their goals. They also understand the importance of unwinding and keeping a healthy mind.

A hard worker also works towards their goals just like a smart worker, but they might lack the traits of analytical thinking, problem-solving, or delegation.

I am a worker focused on results and do not hesitate to ask for help to complete my work. Upper management described me as a smart worker, having successfully led my team to finish projects on time.

In addition to this, physical health is a personal goal. Therefore I spend an hour in the gym daily trying to work hard enough to stay fit and sharp.

Sample 4

To answer this question, one has to redefine the terms smart work and hard work in today's world. Most consider hard work a physical activity and smart work a mental ability. Although this was true before the Internet age, it no longer holds.

Excellence is all about doing smart work day in and day out. This in itself can be considered as hard work. In this industry, there is a lot of competition. The idea is to deliver fast and the best to the clients.

To keep delivering great work every day is hard work, but my agency has been winning the Best Agency Award for the past few years, and this is a commitment to excellence I carry with me too.

Hence, I am sure I fall into the category of both.

Sample 5

Hard work and smart work are different tools to complete a single task. Or you can say that they are two faces of the same coin!

It depends on the task's duration or the difficulty level, on which a measurable amount of hard work and smart work should be put together!

I have learned to adapt myself accordingly to situations and therefore apply myself. If the deadline is two days away, I am a smart worker. I focus on various aspects of the task, which clients need and which will have long-term impacts. If we have two months to complete a task, we spend time on the details and work hard to gain results.

Hard work always guarantees excellent results but requires more effort and time. I work hard or work smart, depending on the situation.

Sample 6

Whenever I'm assigned a task, I spend time researching the same. Then I will try to break the task into actionable steps and achievable goals.

Later I will think about the alternatives of actionable steps which can yield the same results. It gives me a feeling of being focused and engaged.

As a result, I save time, effort, and better output.

Sample 7

Hard work and smart work are different tools to complete a single task. Or you can say that they are two faces of the same coin! It depends on the task's duration or the difficulty level, on which a measurable amount of hard work and smart work should be put together!

I have learned to adapt myself accordingly to situations and therefore apply myself. If the deadline is two days away, I am a smart worker. I focus on various aspects of the task, which clients need and which will have long-term impacts. If we have two months to complete a task, we spend time on the details and work hard to gain results.

Hard work always guarantees excellent results but requires more effort and time. I work hard or work smart, depending on the situation.

Sample 8

I think the combination of both smart and hard work does wonders.

Considering any smart people who have invented a shortcut for any activity has involved a long period of hard work.

You should never hesitate to work hard, but if there is any possibility that you will effectively give the same result, you prefer doing it.

Planning and prioritizing are required before starting the task.

Sample 9

The difference between hard work and smart work is innovation. I am a creative thinker and love to come up with ideas that streamline the work process.

Whenever I am given a task and know how to do it, I take a step back and consider better possibilities. I buy time from my boss to brainstorm with my team, pool free resources, and develop more efficient solutions.

The last project I was assigned in my current company was similar to one I had done with my previous employer. Instead of starting on it immediately, I tried to find out if there was a faster way to do the same work. Brainstorming with my team introduced me to three new tools, eventually reducing our collective hours. It took me a day to learn the tools, but I ensured we would deliver the work in the future in less time.

I do not work hard blindly and instead keep finding new and improved ways to work smart.

"Success seems to be connected with action. Successful people keep moving. They make mistakes, but they don't quit."

N 2 How Do You Stay Organized At Work?

When you answer questions about being organized, you should show the interviewer that you have a defined, proven system and follow up with specific examples if appropriate. You want to answer confidently and make it sound like time management, task management, and the ability to stay organized are easy for you. When describing how you keep yourself organized, you can mention specific tools and technologies, general strategies, task management software, teamwork/communication, and more. Consider sharing a past example of how you used one of your methods/tactics.

When answering straightforward interview questions like How do you stay organized? , you should avoid being too wordy in your response. I recommend spending about 30 seconds describing your approach to organizing your work and then around 20-30 more seconds giving a brief example. If you don't share an example, spend 30-45 seconds describing your general approach and tools to stay organized at work.

Sample 1

I use our company's internal project management software to track weekly priorities and deadlines. I also create a to-do list each morning to organize the individual day.

For example, last month, I had three urgent projects due the same week. By breaking down the week into smaller chunks and prioritizing each day, I could stay organized and deliver all projects on time.

Sample 2

When I was hired in my last role, I quickly saw that I would handle many tasks and need to use my resources efficiently to succeed.

I used an online calendar and to-do list to track priorities and plan my day and week.

I broke down each major project into smaller pieces, which I found helpful for time management and deciding which tasks are most critical each day.

Sample 3

I use an online calendar and to-do list to keep myself organized. I also like to complete my most critical task right away each morning. That way, I still accomplish my main task if I face unforeseen challenges later in the day.

I've also found that communication skills go hand-in-hand with organizational skills, at least in my last few roles. So I've learned to communicate clearly and promptly with my team and project manager regarding progress, setbacks, deadlines, any unanticipated tasks that I need to address, and more.

I've been able to stay organized and handle a heavy workload, including tight deadlines, by following this approach.

Sample 4

My managers in my past two roles had a very hands-off approach, and I was left to develop my organizational skills and systems.

I enjoyed the challenge and created some great systems to save time, prioritize my most critical tasks, and ensure the other functions that aren't top priorities don't fall through the cracks and get forgotten.

In terms of specific tools, I used a combination of email and Google Calendar, plus automated reminders, email tags, and email folders to organize all of my projects.

I can share some past examples of how this looked for specific projects if you'd like.

Sample 5

In my final year of college, I had several challenging projects, all assigned within a few weeks of each other and all due the same week.

I broke each project down into weekly segments to identify what I'd need to accomplish each week to finish on time. I also used an online calendar to coordinate tasks with team members for my team projects.

I finished the semester with a 4.0 GPA, and my time management and organization were big reasons. I want to try using that same approach when I'm hired for my first full-time role since it worked well for me in college.

I'm also open to learning new methods and using additional tools.

Sample 6

I use various digital tools to help me stay organized and remember important events. I use an online calendar because it makes sharing my calendar and work projects with others so easy.

In the past, I've also used different work management platforms to help me accomplish goals and meet deadlines. I enjoyed using the features that simplify the tracking and reporting process. I even downloaded the corresponding apps on my phone to monitor activity remotely.

Of course, I always have a notepad to write down quick reminders and to-do lists. At the end of my shift, I transfer the details of my handwritten notes into my online calendar.

This ensures I don't miss any important details from the day.

Sample 7

Over the years, I've noticed how important it is to keep track of your time at work. Although multitasking is beneficial in many ways, I've learned that when it comes to challenging work, it is better to focus on one project at a time rather than try to do too many things at once.

When working on a tight deadline, I start my day by making a list of priorities. Then I approach the most challenging work first, then move on to other tasks that don't require the same concentration level.

This helps me work more efficiently throughout the rest of the day. I also try to silence my phone and turn off email notifications during deep work to help me avoid distractions.

Sample 8

I appreciate you taking the time to meet with me today, and I look forward to answering any questions you have for me.

I brought extra copies of my resume should you need them. I also got my creative portfolio, including some of the artwork I created for a recent ad campaign.

While working at Inner Circle, I organized company meetings and events. When my manager started requesting more frequent gatherings, I developed a quick system for booking venues and vendors. Once I had this system using some of my favorite apps and online tools, I could book everything in advance within hours.

My manager was so impressed with my efficiency that he promoted me from marketing assistant to event director.

Sample 9

There are times when priorities change throughout the day, and I must reassess my goals.

Some days I don't get everything I had hoped for, but I've learned that starting fresh the next day is okay.

It's all about having a positive attitude and a willingness to adapt to unexpected changes.

Sample 10

Great question! As a manager, staying organized is vital for me and my team.

I have to say I'm a paper and pen devotee of to-do lists. Every Monday morning, I create a weekly to-do list and keep it with me at all times at work, separated into sections, including one for each of my direct reports, with checkboxes I can easily mark as completed. That helps me get an aerial view of the coming week.

But then, each morning, I like to grab a sticky note and write down the most important items I need to tackle that day to help me focus. Of course, that's always subject to change if someone on my team comes to me with an urgent question or problem, and I try to build in some buffer to account for that, whether they need help talking through a tricky script or could use some backup on a call.

Every month and quarter, I set up a tracker for individual and team sales goals in Google Sheets and update it when any deal is closed. I have a reminder on my calendar to spend some time reviewing the tracker every Friday and making notes on steps to take the following week, whether it's checking in with an account executive who's behind on their individual goal to strategize or taking time to recognize an SDR for how thoughtfully and effectively they're teeing up AEs to succeed with new prospects.

"It's okay to outgrow people who don't grow. Grow tall anyways."

0 1 What Would Your First 30, 60, or 90 Days Look Like In This Role?

Think about what information and aspects of the company and team you'd need to familiarize yourself with and which colleagues you'd want to sit down and talk to. You can also suggest one possible starter project to show you'd be ready to hit the ground running and contribute early on.

For the first 30 days, I will get to know the company first and going to be learning as much as possible, including information on the following:

- What does the company do?
- What are the key processes?
- What does your department do?
- What are the current problems and challenges?
- Where can you help?

Then, during the 60 days, I will start making things happen. From all the info you gathered, suggest a handful (3 to 5) initiatives you could take on:

- Will audit the company email marketing strategy and suggest improvements
- Will help come up with better ad copies for Facebook marketing
- Will help the team with their ongoing marketing initiatives

Within the first 90 days, after already having started making an impact. Describe several things you think are going to be functioning better:

- Online ads are going to be performing better by 10-20%
- Email marketing operations will be more streamlined, taking significantly less eff.

Draft an outline of what you plan to do each month once you get the job. Figure out what you will do at your job and prepare for everything you plan to accomplish during that initial period. If possible, stick to quantifiable results.

Keep the language in your 30-60-90 day plan specific and actionable. Your goals should be specific, measurable, achievable, relevant, and time-bound. Assess each goal for these factors before adding it to your 30-60-90 day plan. Prepare to adjust your goals and actions as needed. Learn and adapt from unsuccessful strategies rather than giving up. At the end of each 30 days, quantify your progress. Use this information to inform your next 30 days of work.

Sample 1

In addition to getting to know the team and getting fully up to speed with the role, there's a lot I want to accomplish during my first three months as editor.

During my first 30 days, I want to understand our blog's editorial goals and use those to create a new blog design.

After 60 days, I want our blog redesign launched and to have at least 50 contributors writing for the website.

After 90 days, I want to switch the efforts from building the team to tracking growth, and I'm hoping that we can have 100,000 unique visitors by then through utilizing our marketing channels and those of our contributors.

Sample 2

I know that Nissan Automobiles has seen a decrease in closed sales contracts over the last six months, and I plan to spring into action immediately.

In my first 30 days, I will complete my training faster than expected by spending extra time learning internal processes on the weekends and evenings.

In the first 60 days, I will have contacted all my new clients and built a rapport with them.

After 90 days, I plan to be exceeding sales targets. You'll be very impressed with my drive and steep learning curve.

Sample 3

Within 30 days, I plan to get to know the people I'll be working with the most and be comfortable with them.

Within 60 days, I plan to have a solid understanding of the industry, the company, and the competitive landscape to hold my own in any conversation about the company.

Within 90 days, I plan to meet my goals.

Sample 4

I am delighted you asked this question because I have created a 30-60-90 day plan based on my understanding of the role.

First, I'll meet with my boss to clearly understand their expectations and the challenges and projects that are most important to address. I will learn what my boss expects from me and how they measure success in the role.

Next, I will meet with team members and co-workers to understand how the position fits the larger team.

Finally, I will take the time to complete training on all aspects of the position so I have the knowledge needed to get to work.

Sample 5

I have brought a 30, 60, and 90-day plan. This plan outlines how I will exceed my targets in the first three months while getting to know my new clients, learning the territory, and gaining knowledge of your products. I am very excited to get started!

Sample 6

I want to focus on getting to know the team well in the initial few days. I believe that great ideas originate in a great team. Hence, the first few days would be spent understanding the team dynamics.

In the first 30 days, I would understand the previous projects and analyze the current ones.

By 60 days, I would prioritize the pending projects to be completed and identify new areas where newer projects could be developed.

By 90 days, I would focus on the team's growth and implement new strategies to increase the customer base by at least twice the number.

Understand what's expected during the first three months on the job.

"Success is a matter of sticking to a set of common sense principles anyone can master."

0 2 What Motivates You?

Every company has a certain work culture, and hiring managers want to be sure that whatever motivates you is in line with the overall persona of the company. Interviewers want to know what drove you to have the kind of profile that will help them judge if you are the right fit for the company. Be as honest as possible. You could mention a few circumstances where you gave your best and try to make sense of what made you so driven to achieve the kind of goals that you did. There's a big difference between the candidate motivated by building teams and establishing strong relationships with co-workers and the candidate whose best day is working independently on a report that improves the company's bottom line. Both candidates bring with them unique advantages.

What Motivates You?

- learning new things
- acquiring new skills
- meeting deadlines, goals, and targets
- coaching others
- improving processes, finding ways to solve problems
- leading a team or being a part of a team
- completing a difficult project
- overcoming challenges
- coming up with creative ideas

Tips:

- Sometimes, the best solution is to be honest. You can say money is your motivational factor, but it should be your last option
- Mention things like Job satisfaction, working towards a goal, contributing to a team effort, or developing your skills. Provide a specific example that supports your response
- Excitement for new challenges
- Quest for personal development

What not to say:

- Do not mention that you are motivated by bragging rights, material things, or fear of being disciplined

Sample 1

I am a very result-oriented person. My primary motivation is to achieve the desired result. While I enjoy working on the project independently, I am particularly motivated by the buzz of working in a team. Working closely with others who share the same common goal is very exciting. I also like to take on the challenge and rise to that challenges as part of a concerted team effort.

Sample 2

Primarily, my ability to work hard and deliver results motivates me. But subsequent recognition of my efforts encourages me to put more effort into the following tasks.

Sample 3

Responsibility toward work motivates me the most. My aim within any company is to move up to greater levels of commitment to achieve each goal with higher and better responsibilities.

Sample 4

Many things motivate me. My goal is to be the best of what I can be, which often inspires me to exceed my expectations. When I see myself being productive every day, it motivates me to continue.

Sample 5

Meeting the set target within an assigned deadline motivates me the most. When I do so, I get a sense of accomplishment and fulfillment. Coupled with an award, I feel all the more motivated.

Overall, I like to achieve milestones, so I can look back at them and say, Yes, that was my achievement. Visible results also motivate me.

Sample 6

Results drive me. I like it when I have a concrete goal to meet and enough time to figure out a strong strategy for accomplishing it. At my last job, our yearly goals were very aggressive, but I worked with my manager and the rest of my team to figure out a month-by-month strategy for meeting the year-end numbers. It was a real thrill to accomplish that.

Sample 7

I love working as a part of a team. I enjoy discussing ways to move forward with teammates and respectfully debating others to ensure we are moving in the right direction. On top of that, I take pride in my work, and it is humbling whenever I see a product or service being used in the real world.

Sample 8

I have always wanted to ensure that my company's clients get the best customer service I can offer. I feel it's important, both to me personally and for the company and the clients, to provide a positive customer experience. My drive to constantly develop my customer service skills is why I earned top sales at my company two quarters in a row.

Sample 9

I'm motivated by digging into data. Give me a spreadsheet and questions; I'm eager to determine what drives the numbers. At my current position, I prepare the monthly analytics report around sales. The data from these reports help drive and determine how the company charts its next steps and makes sales goals for the following months. Being able to provide that essential information is motivating.

Sample 10

I enjoy flexing my imagination and creative muscles. Art and modern design were my first true love, and my appreciation and devotion to superior artistic direction continue just as strongly now. My adoration for creativity dictates every other aspect of my life, and I'd love for it to be used in my career, too.

"The secret to success is to know something nobody else knows."

P 1 Problem-Solving Skills

Problem-solving questions can vary across industries, but in most cases, they focus on how logically and effectively you can analyze a problem and figure out a plausible solution to that problem. Also known as analytical skills, these questions help a company understand how a candidate analyses and solves a complex problem when faced with one. They may ask some carefully designed questions that can tell them about the candidate's approach towards difficult situations and how result-oriented they can be at work. They may want to understand if your logical problem-solving process involves gathering information, analyzing the information, and making decisions based on what you have found.

Sample 1

When I face a problem, first, I look for examples of how others have solved the same problem. This research equips me with various approaches to solving the problem and helps me select the one that best suits me and the organization. Then, I determine how to solve the problem, which involves communicating with my managers and colleagues.

The interviewer is trying to know how resourceful you can be when employers assign you demanding tasks. They want to understand how you face challenging situations, test your accountability, and if you are a professional who may bring or solve problems.

Sample 2

I was a junior sales executive in my previous organization and progressed to area sales manager despite not having the proper training. With little training, it compelled me to figure out things primarily by myself. This exercise trained me to take up responsibilities that were sometimes beyond my job description. Now, when I am assigned a task for which I lack the necessary knowledge, I gain an understanding of it on my own and give my best to accomplish it.

Sample 3

When I was working as a showroom manager, a customer came to pick up a car he had booked a few months ago. When I checked the day's delivery list, I found that someone from the team had accidentally delivered the car to another customer. I quickly called up my contacts in other showrooms to arrange for the same car model, and within a couple of hours, I got it to the showroom and delivered it to the customer.

Sample 4

When I encounter an agitated customer, I stay calm and use an approach that doesn't upset them further. Next, I ask them why they are dissatisfied, which helps me gather all the details to solve the problem. Once I have understood what has gone wrong, I assure the customer that I and my team may take all the steps to fix the concern swiftly. I even give the customer regular updates to know their issue is getting resolved adequately.

Sample 5

Before I present my recommendation, I would ask my supervisor to share the company's budget and the team's requirements. Once I have the information, I will start reading about the productivity software options that suit the team and the budget. Apart from features and price, I would also consider how future-proof the software is so that the company does not spend on other software soon. Finally, I will give the supervisor my top three software options with all their pros and cons.

Sample 6

My first step is to make sure that I carefully examine the pros and cons and what each of them can cause. Next, I contemplate the obstacles I or my team can face because of the cons. If they can hinder achieving targets, then the approach may not be practical. Then I consider how the pros outweigh the cons and what positive results they can deliver. If they outdo the cons in terms of accomplishments, I will prefer to pursue them and deal with the impediments as they come my way.

Sample 7

You have been asked to schedule a rush project but cannot complete the work you need to since you require information from another unavailable colleague. How would you deal with the situation?

The best option here would be to reassess the situation. Can you continue with any other project elements until your colleague returns? If this isn't an option, you should explore every avenue to try and contact them or someone in their team who could help.

Sample 8

You are working on a project, and halfway through, you realize that you have made a significant mistake that may require you to restart the project to resolve it. How would you approach this so you still meet the deadline?

Stop what you are doing and evaluate the mistake. Is it small enough to resolve without taking too much time? If so, resolve the mistake and move on. Alternatively, if there is no other option than to rework the project (which may impact meeting the deadline), the first thing to do is notify your supervisor. You may need to reschedule your day or work longer to finish the project and meet the deadline.

Sample 9

How would you deal with a customer who wasn't happy with your service, even though you haven't done anything wrong and the customer has made a mistake?

No matter how upset, abrupt, or angry the customer is, it is up to the employee to make sure they are treated with respect. The best way to do this is to be attentive and show genuine concern for their problem. It is the role of an employee to turn a negative situation into a positive. If your efforts still fail, notify your supervisor as a final option.

"The world is full of nice people. If you can't find one, be one."

P 2 What Is Your Management Style?

You can find many different categorizations of management styles. Sometimes it is hard to understand what this or that category means. A job interview is no school exam. Hiring managers expect to hear how you manage people; in an ideal case, they want to hear about some illustration of your style.

Results matter the most for managers. Long-term results over the short term, to be more precise. Regardless of whether you prefer to lead the team with an iron fist or let your people do whatever they want (or anything in between), as long as it works for you, you achieve your goals, and people do not leave the company under your leadership.

Sample 1

Let's say you have managerial experience. Think about what's worked best for you in the past. Go into a bit of detail to personalize your answer.

I assess the situation and the team before deciding what action to take to get results. There are times when the health and safety of the team depends on clear instructions.

Investing in the long-term development of employees is the best way to achieve sustainable results.

Sample 2

Even though the candidate has no managerial experience, one can share a leadership success story.

I have not yet had the opportunity to find out what my particular managerial style would be. At the same time, I've found that the best managers have a versatile supervising style. From my experience, I work best with managers who pay attention to individual needs.

My last manager was a good example. She used slow periods to coach workers who needed more instruction. When things sped up, she gave clear instructions and took on tasks herself if necessary.

Although I've never been a manager, I took on several leadership roles as a student. I was the team captain of our academic team for two years. I ensured each team member knew what they were responsible for before matches. At the same time, we often switched roles depending on who felt strongest. I took a democratic approach to leadership.

I motivated the team by encouraging constructive feedback after matches. We won districts both years and were invited to nationals during my senior year.

Sample 3

For me, the best approach to management is to switch back and forth between styles.

I like to encourage the team to bond. A good manager invests in building a close-knit team that works well together. Of course, this managerial style only pays off in the long run. I reassign tasks or pick up the slack myself for more immediate crises. I use threats and negative motivation only as a last resort.

Sample 4

I was in charge of a team of 15+ people working across departments. The team started to miss deadlines. I found that miscommunication was causing some interdepartmental hostility.

To resolve the situation, I organized a team-building activity. I gave the team several fun, communication-based tasks. After each game, I mixed the members until everyone had worked together at least once.

Ultimately, we discussed what forms of communication worked and what didn't. I then led a brainstorming session about how they could use these skills around the office. The hostility between the teams evaporated, and productivity doubled. We even beat our sales target that month by 15%.

Sample 5

I trust my team. I start every project by ensuring that I give clear directions and outline our overall goals, but I make a real effort not to micromanage. I prefer to remain hands-off when it comes to individual tasks, but at the same time, I'm always available for help, guidance, and assistance when needed.

I like to know what's going on with regular informal check-ins. Still, I try not to make people feel like I'm breathing down their necks or forcing everyone to sacrifice valuable work time to hold unnecessary team meetings.

A few years ago, I was on a large software project with five people working on a separate piece of code that would eventually be combined into one large program. Rather than have people start and stop work to participate in group sessions. I set up a communication board that allowed us to communicate as a group or individually instantly. I also included a status update section where we could post what we were all working on and how it was going.

It allowed me to stay updated on every aspect of the project without being intrusive and gave us all a way to work together. It also allowed anyone to reach me anytime with issues and problems, allowing us to solve them quickly. The entire program was finished on time, and the board was such a successful idea that I now use it with every project I work on.

Sample 6

Once, I had to finish a project with a tight deadline while shorthanded. The first order of business was to redistribute the workload.

I held a meeting, and we mapped out the project. After delegating most of them to myself, I asked for volunteers to take on the extra tasks. I opted for a pace-setting managerial style. I set a fast pace, taking work from team members who couldn't perform and assigning it to others. We finished the project in a state of exhaustion. But the team admired that I rolled up my sleeves and joined them.

My supervisor asked me to turn the experience into a workshop for others. Later, the project won an industry award that made the team proud.

Sample 7

In my experience as a manager, I try to avoid micromanaging and let my employees work independently. At the same time, my employees always know they can come to me if they need help on a project or are having difficulties. I like for everyone to feel involved so everyone can provide input when making a business decision.

I can recall a time when my team was brainstorming ideas for a possible fundraising campaign. Everyone was involved in suggesting ideas, and we decided by taking a vote from everyone in the office.

Sample 8

There's no one management style I use all the time. I adapt depending on the employee and their needs. For example, some employees like having daily guidance and support, while others prefer to check in less often.

I oversee a team of contractors working on a project at my current job. One of them sends me Slack messages a few times daily, but she consistently puts out good work because she knows what's expected of her. But other contractors do great stuff daily without my input, and I'm happy to leave them to it.

I take the time to communicate big-picture goals and talk to each person I'm in charge of at least once a week. That led to a 78% contractor retention rate, a significant improvement from the sub-50% we saw before I took over the project.

Sample 9

At my last job as a Marketing Director, I was able to start with a vision for carrying out a content marketing push for our brand.

I brought it to the marketing team, and with their input and lots of revision, we came up with a definitive vision.

By communicating this to everyone from the outset, we were able to turn the project around a month early and 10% under budget. An excellent starting vision is a powerful thing.

Sample 10

I believe that a good leader is motivating and encouraging.

I always work to get myself out of my comfort level and do the same with my co-workers to guide them through this challenging task if necessary.

I accomplished this with a content writer I once mentored. I encouraged her to write long content on topics they had little idea about. This led to her becoming my strongest research writer on the marketing team.

"If you can't do anything about it, let it go. Don't be a prisoner to things you can't change."

Q 1 What You Think Are The Most Challenging Aspects Of The Job?

Choosing aspects of the job that aren't critical to your specific role is usually best. For example, if you're a journalist applying for a position as a web editor, you might mention you're working on improving your photojournalism or video skills. Don't say that proofreading or writing copy will be your biggest challenge because, as a web editor, these are the position's core responsibilities.

Selecting a knowledge or skill area, you lack is generally more advisable than choosing a personality trait that would be hard to change. For example, if you're applying for a sales position, you would not want to mention that reaching out to new people makes you nervous. Instead, you might mention that you have modest skills in PowerPoint but would be glad to take workshops or complete online tutorials to upgrade your skills.

Mention a fundamental strength you possess that would help you overcome the challenge. For example, you could say you've always been a quick learner.

Sample 1

One of my biggest challenges will be adjusting to the new workflow and creating a new type of report to present to clients.

I plan to ask many questions when preparing my first report. I'll also ask a colleague to review the report before sharing it with the client.

Sample 2

I've previously used Microsoft Word processing and presentation software exclusively and haven't used Google's online equivalents.

Although I'll have to learn a whole new set of keyboard shortcuts, I'll devote time to reading blog posts that walk me through the differences between the two types of software, and I'll watch online tutorials.

Sample3

I'm excited about scheduling an offsite conference, but it'll be challenging.

On the plus side, although I haven't organized large corporate events before, I have planned personal events, including a 100-person family reunion and team-wide holiday dinners for 200 people.

If I get this job, one of the first things I'll do is meet with the person who organized last year's offsite event to get pointers. I'll also touch base with a former colleague who orchestrated offsite conferences for her company.

Sample 4

I cleared the GMAT on the first attempt and obtained the second national rank. It is my biggest accomplishment because I prepared for the exam and worked full-time to support my family.

My rank has made me believe in the virtues of hard work and a positive, goal-oriented outlook in life, and I intend to carry these with me as I begin a career in Hospital Management.

Sample 5

For me, one of my bigger challenges will be adjusting to the new CRM software and creating new types of reports to provide to my clients. I had a similar situation before and managed to get to know all systems in and out within the first month. Furthermore, I plan to ask many questions during the process. I'll also ask the manager to discuss the reports before sharing them with clients.

Sample 6

The most challenging aspect of my last job was troubleshooting some of the older technology. We needed some serious upgrades, but they weren't in the budget. Learning how to work around this problem was quite a challenge, but I learned how by referring to old manuals and online forums. I became one of the stronger users of this program in our entire office! I quickly became the go-to person when anyone had questions about the technology.

Sample 7

I get a lot of energy from thinking I will lead the team and set new sales goals, but it will be challenging! However, although I have not managed an entire team by myself yet, I have coached and mentored co-workers to help them develop as professionals. If I get this job, one of the first things I will do is meet with the other managers to discuss how they run their teams. I always enjoyed talking to colleagues about strategies to make the company perform as well as possible.

Sample 8

My previous role was with a small agency where budgets were always a concern for the clients. Although I liked the clients, they were usually independent businesses with less than ten employees. They had a hard time thinking big-picture. I overcame this by developing a questionnaire to address their greatest pain points and needs for their business. I would then focus on their small goals versus what I felt their company could be.

Some business owners are more comfortable being comfortable than ruling the world, which is okay! I just needed to wrap my marketing brain around that.

Sample 9

At my previous job, a colleague left the company suddenly. Unfortunately, this colleague had a major role in an important project. We didn't have time to replace her, so I was asked to take over her job so that we could stay on deadline. I had to get up to speed quickly, doing her job and my own. We completed the project on time, and the client was happy.

"Yesterday, I was clever and wanted to change the world. Today I am wise, so I am changing myself."

Q 2 How Do You Prioritize Tasks?

In today's fast-paced work environment with conflicting and competing deadlines, prioritizing your tasks and managing your time is critical. Future employers would be interested to know how you prioritize your work during the interview and ensure that assigned tasks are completed on time.

Prioritization includes estimating the time, effort, and resources needed to accomplish a task. Walk the interviewer through your logical thought process for planning your work.

Your prioritization plan can include listing all your tasks, reviewing your to-do list, and identifying major deadlines and priorities. Re-check the inventory regularly during the day and cross out items completed. Re-balance your list as appropriate. Your to-do or prioritization list can be in electronic format, hard copy, or both. Meeting with your boss regularly to align priorities is a good strategy. During these types of meetings, outline the major tasks on your plate. Likewise, find out the assignments that are of the highest priority to your boss now.

Methods for managing your workflow include calendars, diaries, spreadsheets, notepads, projects, and work scheduling software and applications.

Good practices in managing priorities include setting up reminders, assigning start and end dates for major work, clarifying due dates when given a new task, delegating, figuring out typical and unforeseen delays and hold-ups, and knowing when to ask for help.

Other methods include grouping similar or related tasks and doing them together whenever possible, working on one item at a time, and prioritizing tasks in a workflow where colleagues are waiting for your input to push the task to the next step.

Moreover, breakdown large tasks into smaller activities and assign a mini deadline for each action. Furthermore, you could categorize your to-do list into three major categories: high priority, medium priority, and low priority.

Besides, you can discuss steps that you have proactively taken to improve your prioritization skills. For example, you are attending time management courses, reading online tutorials, reading books, and learning from co-workers about their methods of prioritizing their tasks.

Sample 1

As a Procurement Specialist, I manage critical purchasing deadlines from multiple departments, communicate with hundreds of suppliers, and resolve purchasing issues.

Daily I write down a to-do list of all my tasks.

I write my list on spreadsheets with different tabs for each day.

I then review the list and identify high-priority items with upcoming deadlines.

I also have a daily check-in meeting with my boss to learn their priorities and readjust my tasks accordingly.

Before working on each task, I mentally estimate how long it will take.

When emergencies and unforeseen deadlines arise, I quickly jump to address those and reorganize my priority list accordingly.

I review all completed tasks at the end of each day and prepare a to-do list for the following day.

Relating how you prioritize key tasks of the job can demonstrate how you fit the job's requirements and understand the expectations of the role.

Sample 2

I prioritize my work according to company objectives and what is expected of me as an office administrator. I organize my workload to reflect my most urgent priorities, such as corresponding with clients and communicating team updates. I follow my urgent tasks with important organizational tasks like creating the topic outlines for our monthly team conferences. When I prioritize my work this way, I still have room for any changes in priorities while maintaining a healthy balance between my work and personal life.

Sample 3

I am used to working under tight deadlines, so I set my most urgent tasks at the top of my to-do list every morning when I get to work. Then, I establish a clear deadline for myself that's usually a day before company due dates. Recently, I had to shift my workload to accommodate an urgent product order. The client wanted custom modifications to the product completed in a week, but our standard lead time for implementing changes is around 10 to 14 days.

Sample 4

I communicated with my production department and manufacturing team to implement urgent changes in the production timeline. These adjustments allowed us to ship the product to the client on time, effectively reducing the time it took to apply the customizations by three days.

Sample 5

Every morning when I arrive at work, I look over my company task sheet to review any new development projects I have. Since some of my software projects can take longer than others, I communicate with clients about their expectations for completion. I use the client's input to help me organize my most urgent tasks and set deadlines for completing projects. Then, I create a document to share with my team lead so they know which tasks I'm working through and which tasks I'm moving toward the end of the week.

Sample 6

I prioritize my workload by first communicating with senior analysts if there are any urgent developments. Then, I create a to-do list based on our company shareholders' business objectives. Since analyzing risk and costs are typically among my most urgent tasks, I usually complete my risk and cost analysis documentation assignments first. Once completed, I collaborate again with senior analysts to ensure my work meets my supervisors' and stakeholders' expectations.

Sample 7

I start with a checklist of all tasks and then sort them between urgent (priority) and important (secondary). If a task is unclear, I acquire more information before rating it. New tasks being assigned to the project are evaluated and then added to the appropriate list.

Sample 8

If I encounter a problematic area, I ask for suggestions from others (team members, supervisor, manager), then re-evaluate the project and make changes as needed.

Sample 9

If the estimated deadline is unclear, I'll evaluate the tasks and then discuss the situation with my manager to make suggestions or recommendations.

"Try not to become a man of success but rather become a man of value."

R 1 How Do You Deal With Conflicts In Your Team

When you manage a team of people, you can't always ensure they'll get along. Given competing interests, needs, and agendas, you might even have two people who fervently disagree. Ideally, you'll be able to coach your colleagues to talk to each other and resolve their conflict without involving you, making clear that their disagreement harms them and the organization. But that's not always possible. In these situations, we believe intervening is important, not as a boss but as a mediator. You won't be a neutral, independent mediator since you have some stake in the outcome. Still, you're likely more effective in meeting everybody's interests, yours, theirs, and the organization's.

Sample 1

I will address the issue head-on and open communication when there is conflict. Hearing the problem before deciding on a solution, and perhaps most importantly, hearing the parties out, is most important. I believe in allowing the stakeholders to have a say in what they think will work best for them and then working together to create a solution that will work best for everyone.

Sample 2

I have strong conflict management skills, and in my current position, I have had to exercise those skills from time to time. We are in a high-stress, highly commissioned work environment, which can cause a lot of unnecessary conflict among the team. When a dispute arises, I like to deal with it swiftly, openly, and with poise. Transparency and openness are how

I lead my team, so I will call a group meeting where we express concerns and get it all out on the table.

Sample 3

I think a bit of conflict is good for a team. We all have a right to voice our opinions and must know disagreeing is okay. As we disagree, we find new spaces for growth and new directions because of those uncomfortable conversations.

Conflict can be very beneficial if it remains in check and everyone behaves as adults and treats one another and our differing opinions with respect.

Sample 4

In a sales environment, competition is necessary and integral to the organization's fiber. However, it can prove problematic, especially among those on the same team who are supposed to work collaboratively but ultimately are competing.

On one occasion, the two buyers who reported to me verbally argued. I calmly pulled them both off the floor to a private room. We were able to get to the heart of the issue. It boiled down to one feeling the other was trying to be his manager when he had no authority over him. We solved the problem by communicating job tasks and dividing power.

Sample 5

Some time ago, I had an unhappy patient who felt my fee was too high.

Even though she was happy with her treatment, she refused to pay for her service before leaving. Rather than cause a scene around my other patients, I asked her to leave and not to return. I took the loss and moved on. Some battles just aren't worth fighting.

Sample 6

One of my coworkers had a bad attitude and kept snapping at people on the team one day. We must always work together, even if one of us is having a bad day.

I pulled him aside and asked what was going on. I listened and comforted him and then gave him a pep talk.

I told him we needed him on the team and that he was doing great. The rest of the day went much more smoothly!

Sample 7

In my previous role as a Service Station Manager, I ensured the delivery of excellent customer service by training my team to be positive-minded and encouraging to everyone around them.

Customers can tell when someone wants to help them versus being forced to. We created a friendly and welcoming environment that our regular customers greatly appreciated.

Sample 8

I resolved a conflict just last week between two of my kitchen helpers. They disagreed about the schedule and booked time off. I resolved this by sitting down with them individually and then together. We came down to the basis of the issue and fixed it quickly through strong communication.

Sample 9

I had a situation with a Provider who over-dosed a patient and miscalculated the patient's weight.

After a professional discussion, we realized it was a miscommunication, and the Dr. misread a patient's weight. He may not have admitted guilt, but he walked away and didn't raise his voice after I brought the error to his attention.

Sample 10

There are always two sides to every story, which is why it's so important to me to remain as neutral and open-minded as possible whenever I hear of conflict between teammates.

I was in a situation a few years ago where two team members were unhappy with each other, rather than letting it irritate or ignoring it with the hope that they could work it out themselves.

I sat with them individually and asked them to explain what was happening. We discussed reasonable and professional solutions that worked for both parties and resolved the matter.

"If you do what you always did, you will get what you always got."

R 2 How Do You Delegate Tasks To Employees?

As a manager, you must delegate responsibility as effectively and efficiently as possible. That's also why the interviewer wants to know how you make sure to do this and how you did this in the past. A good manager understands how to accomplish tasks that need to be done by their team. You need to demonstrate that you can keep the focus on the bigger picture.

Sample 1

My previous management experience taught me to consider each team member's strengths and responsibilities before delegating tasks. I'm involved in multiple projects as a manager, and whenever I'm engaged in a new project, I talk to each team member individually and the team as a unit.

I discuss what I think they can take on as a team and individually and ask them how I can support them in achieving our goals. I select a project manager and delegate the day-to-day tasks to him. That person is then responsible for coordinating daily tasks while I do regular check-ins and supporting the team when and where necessary to ensure we reach our targets.

Sample 2

My management experience made me conclude that delegating tasks is necessary to succeed, no matter how small or big a team or group might be. I've done many successful projects with different teams, and the only reason for these successes was through careful planning, organizing, and team structuring.

My strength lies in recognizing the potential and abilities of each team member and delegating tasks to reach optimum team performance. There are two reasons for this conclusion. The first one is that delegating tasks helps me to get all the tasks at hand done and finalized within the set deadlines.

The second reason is that delegating tasks allows your team members to work up to their full potential. This way, employees can develop themselves as professionals and climb the company ladder.

Sample 3

In my previous job, I was in charge of the sales department and was responsible for several smaller teams. We were invited to pitch to a new client for a long-term contract at a certain time. This was a big deal for the company and meant several years of additional turnover. As I was responsible for this pitch's success, I understood there was no room for error.

I composed a team of the most experienced employees and selected them based on their qualities and strengths to balance the team. We planned and set goals and milestones with the team to work on the pitch. After that, I delegated tasks based on each team member's knowledge and experience levels. Also, I hired a project manager to carefully monitor the progress daily and report to me on the milestone progress.

Because I distributed the responsibilities according to experience and knowledge levels, everyone on the team thoroughly understood their responsibilities and the importance of the project. The team delivered everything on time without requiring intense oversight on an ongoing basis.

We finished our pitch beforehand and provided the client with everything he requested. The client told us that he was impressed by our efforts, and we landed the contract. This was an excellent achievement for the team as it was an effort that could not have been made without the people on it.

Sample 4

I prefer to delegate tasks based on the aptitude of each team member for the task at hand. Before delegating, I like to discuss the project with my team. We break it down and determine what needs to get done and who is the best person for each task.

I review each assignment personally and ensure the assigned individual has the knowledge and skills to complete the task in time.

Sample 5

A few years ago, I was brought in to replace a project manager in a store that was, for lack of a better word, failing. The sales team was unmotivated, the customer complaints were a mile long, and the entire store was dirty and disorganized.

We closed the shop for 24 hours so I could sit down with the entire team and discuss what was happening. Within an hour of talking to the employees, I discovered that the previous manager had spent their time pitting team members against each other, scheduled work hours and tasks based on who they liked, not what the employees had been hired to do, and had made working there miserable for most of the employees.

We completely restructured the entire team based on each person's strengths and skills. We also spent the rest of the day cleaning and reorganizing the store. The next day we opened with everyone in their new roles and with new tasks assigned. Within a week, we were doing better numbers than had been done the month prior, and within six months, the store had become one of the top-performing stores in the area.

It made me feel so good knowing that I had helped turn the store around, and all it had taken was listening to what the employees had to say and delegating tasks and responsibilities based on their skills and strengths.

"The ones who are crazy enough to think they can change the world are the ones who do."

S 1 How Do You Handle Stress And Pressure?

With competition increasing by leaps and bounds, stress and pressure naturally come uninvited. Understanding what causes stress and how to tackle it for a flawless performance is extremely important. Nowadays, interviewers are keen on learning how working professionals handle stress and pressure, making it one of the most frequently asked interview questions.

Sample 1

I was assigned a vital project at the last minute in my previous organization. And, since my seniors were busy with their respective projects

I was left to handle the project all on my own. Although it initially seemed daunting, I calmed down and chalked out a plan, which helped me tackle the project and efficiently meet my deadline.

With focus and perseverance, I completed the task, and that too on time. The boss was also much pleased with the results.

Sample 2

I believe that stress can be of two types, good and bad. It can be universally accepted that too much stress has never benefited anyone.

However, stress can help push our limits and produce better results. As for me, I believe a healthy amount of stress provides me with enough challenges to stay focused and get out of my comfort zone. This, in turn, helps me to achieve better results.

Over the years, I have developed this habit of assigning deadlines to myself, which has helped me consistently submit assignments on time.

Sample 3

While handling a team, it is imperative to be observant of its dynamics. I understand the difference between good and bad stress. So, whenever I feel that the team's dynamics are changing under excessive stress, I communicate with my teammates about it. When in stress, you must maintain calm to get your work done.

So, I prefer to listen to and check in on their concerns. After all, a team is known for its group efforts. So, a happy and stress-free team will produce better work.

Sample 4

Given the extreme competition nowadays, I understand that stress will come uninvited.

Therefore, I engage in other exercises to refresh myself and avoid the negative energy that stress brings.

I think exercise plays a significant role in handling stress as it helps lift one's mood and helps handle problems better with better reflexes.

Sample 5

I believe your lifestyle profoundly impacts how you react to workplace stress. Therefore, I have made it a habit to engage in outdoor sports and yoga to keep stress at bay.

On the work front, I like to keep myself organized. My deadlines are always marked on a calendar and put on my desk. This helps me remember the projects' deadlines and produce better results.

Sample 6

While I can't say I enjoy stress, I must admit that handling stressful situations has taught me a lot about prioritization and communication.

In my most recent job, I had to answer two supervisors who occasionally assigned me conflicting tasks. Rather than trying to tackle both simultaneously and ending up overwhelmed and stressed, I sat down with my supervisors and discussed which tasks were more urgent and could be done later. We worked out a game plan that allowed me to organize what needed to get done based on priority.

We used that to build a list of assignments. Not only could I finish both tasks quickly and efficiently, but it gave me a lot of satisfaction every time I checked things off the assignment list. Now I'm all about lists and making sure I'm correctly prioritizing tasks, and as a result, I've found I can handle much bigger workloads at a fraction of the stress level I had experienced before.

Sample 7

As the head of a large corporation, I can't afford to let stress affect my ability to do my job. I have a lot of people answering to me, and stress from my level can filter down through the entire company and cause many issues.

I've learned that prioritization and organization are the best ways for me to help minimize stress. Of course, things still come up unexpectedly, and I've found the best way to manage that stress is to step back, look at the big picture, and see why this issue is causing the stress I'm trying to solve.

A few years ago, we lost one of our major suppliers. We had a massive order to fill, and our supplier was key to ensuring the order was correct. Millions of dollars were at stake. I'm sure you can imagine it was stressful for me.

Rather than panic, I brought in my upper-level management team, and we sat down for a full day of problem-solving. Everyone had an opportunity to offer solutions and workarounds. By the end of the day, we had not only found a new supplier but had managed to reduce the overall cost of the final product as a result.

It was a huge win for us all, and I could not have done it alone. That roundtable has become a regular part of my problem-solving process, and now, whenever I start to feel stressed from any part of my job, I call in my team of experts to see how we can make things work.

"Knowledge is being aware of what you can do. Wisdom is knowing when not to do it."

S 2 What Was Your Biggest Failure, and How Did You Handle It?

What is your biggest failure? can impress upon interviewers your resiliency and ability to turn failure into a learning opportunity. Choose situations where you took responsibility for your failure, learned from it, and took steps to avoid recurrences of similar failures. Interviewers understand that no one is perfect. What they want to understand is whether you are self-aware enough to acknowledge your shortcomings and whether you are someone who can learn from your missteps. Failures also tell a lot about who you are as an employee and whether you are comfortable taking smart risks and pushing beyond your comfort zone to achieve goals. Keep the tone positive, and talk about how you rectified your mistakes. Emphasize what you learned from that failure, which has helped you avoid repeating the same mistake.

Sample 1

I was managing a project where a new client wanted a large number of unique product descriptions written to improve the SEO ranking of their site. Because they were a new client and I wanted to impress them with the results we could produce, I assured them we could return it to them in two weeks. I thought this was doable with multiple writers working on the project, but it took an extra week, and they were unhappy.

We apologized and reassured them that the mistake wouldn't happen again. I realized that it's far better to under-promise and over-deliver.

The client isn't upset when you are clear about the timeline from the beginning. Problems arise when you can't meet promised deadlines. I used this experience to be more cautious in managing client expectations. For the next client project I worked on, I included extra time for unforeseen circumstances and told them we would deliver in four weeks. We delivered in three, and they couldn't have been more thrilled.

Sample 2

I took a job where I was responsible for building a sales team that would fix the major revenue problems the company was having. I was confident in my abilities and certain I could accomplish the goal. After arriving, I realized the issues were not just in revenue but in how the company was organized. Within one month, I knew I couldn't make the impact I anticipated.

I briefly considered quitting when I knew I wouldn't come close to the sales goals I promised, but instead, I decided to focus on the things I could control. I met with the company's executives and altered our sales goals for the year. We also decided to scale back the size of my team and bring on a consultant to fix some of the company's deeper problems. Being in this situation reminded me of the importance of focusing on what you can control and collaborating to find solutions to complex problems. I also learned a hard lesson in humility and not jumping in and making promises before fully understanding the scope of the problem.

Sample 3

Several years ago, my supervisor tasked me interviewing, hiring, and training an entry-level person to join our customer service team. I chose to hire someone who seemed eager to learn and, based on past work experiences, seemed to have a lot of potential. After checking their social media sites, I had a few concerns but hired them anyway. I quickly learned it was a mistake and that their social media activity strongly indicated their work behavior. They were highly dramatic, had a poor attitude, and impacted the entire team until I had to fire them.

The experience taught me how important every hiring decision is, from senior staff to interns. Each person impacts company morale and culture. It also taught me not to rush to make hiring decisions and get feedback if I have concerns about a candidate. I've learned to trust my intuition more. However, it's a lesson I'm glad I learned earlier in my career.

Sample 4

I believe my biggest failure was when the team that I was a part of couldn't succeed in completing Project A.

The primary problem was that the whole team was complacent, as we thought it was an easy target to achieve. But, the project cost us a lot when it didn't work out. I realized we didn't go that extra mile to achieve what we wanted.

Henceforth, I have always made sure that I remain alert and keep my eyes open to the realities of a situation. In fact, on our next project, although the team was putting in exemplary efforts, I knew the team had the potential to achieve that winner factor.

I stepped up and motivated my teammates to push even harder, and this project got us esteemed recognition in the company.

Sample 5

In college, I worked as a door-to-door outside salesperson at a solar company. Outside of knocking on residential doors, I constantly thought of new ways to bring in business.

I developed a PowerPoint presentation and walked around to local businesses sharing a partnership idea.

Although the logistics sounded good, and I even received a few stores interested in partnering with me, I did not run the idea past my company first.

Sadly, they shut it down. I quickly learned that even great ideas could be turned down, and there was absolutely nothing that I could do about it.

In the future, I will consult with my company on any new ideas before creating a plan.

Failure is inevitable. It's what you learn from your failure that will define you.

Sample 6

I have faced many hurdles in my career, and I feel that failures change your personality. The most important loss of my life was at the start of my career. I joined the reputed media agency and was part of ten team members. At that time, I was entirely new to the corporate culture. What I learned from my working environment was to be disciplined and hard-working. I was responsible for interacting with big clients and understanding their requirements. Being a fresher, I did not pay much attention to the details of the project. Instead, I focused only on my ethics and discipline. My poor listening skills led me to lose one of the most significant projects of the organization. It had a negative impact on my appraisal, and I realized what I lacked. I discussed the issue with my manager, who helped me learn how to handle projects effectively. This project made me realize that, along with specific essential values, you need to keep your focus and attention on listening and communicating effectively.

Sample 7

Last semester, I had two weeks to work on a big assignment. Since the due date seemed so far away, I put off starting it for a few days. That was a big mistake. I had to do two weeks' worth of work in four days while also trying to find time to study for exams and presentations in other classes. My final grade on the project was a low C, plus I failed a test for another course.

Though I got a passing grade, I know I could have done much better if I had managed my time more wisely. The experience taught me about the consequences of procrastination. Since then, I have tried to devote enough time to each of my assignments. Now I can take my time and do my best on all my projects.

Sample 8

My biggest failure was getting fired from a previous job because I lost my temper with a customer. I was already in a bad mood when I went to work that day, so when an angry shopper came in with a complaint, I made the awful choice to give them a bit of an attitude. Eventually, we shouted at each other in the middle of the store, and a manager had to step in and send me home.

Up to that point, I had never been fired from a job. It was embarrassing to admit that I had acted that way, making it hard to get another customer service position. To keep my temper under control, I started doing deep breathing exercises to calm down intense situations. I watch a few funny video clips before work every day to put myself in a happy mood.

"Success is knowing your purpose in life, growing to reach your maximum potential, and sowing seeds that benefit others."

T 1 Can You Tell Me About a Time When You Had To Solve a Challenging Problem?

This one might be your best-case scenario in the land of problem-solving questions. It lets you choose your problem-solving examples to highlight, putting you in complete control.

When you choose an example, choose one relevant to what you'll face in the role. The closer the match, the better the answer is in the eyes of the hiring manager.

When you're answering this question, quantify the details. This gives your answer critical context and scale, showcasing the accomplishment's degree of challenge and strength. That way, your answer is powerful, compelling, and, above all, thorough.

Sample 1

While working as a mobile telecom support specialist for a large organization, we had to transition our MDM service from one vendor to another within 45 days.

Devices had to be gathered from the headquarters and satellite offices across the state, which was challenging even without the tight deadline.

I approached the situation by identifying the location assignment of all personnel within the organization, enabling me to estimate transit times for receiving the devices. Next, I timed out how many devices I could update daily. Together, this allowed me to create a general timeline.

After that, I coordinated with each location, expressing the urgency of adhering to deadlines and scheduling bulk shipping options. While there were occasional bouts of resistance, I worked with location leaders to calm concerns and facilitate action.

While performing all the updates was daunting, my approach to organizing the event made it successful. Ultimately, the transition was finished five days before the deadline, exceeding many expectations.

Sample 2

When I first began in a supervisory role, I had trouble setting down my contributor hat. I tried to keep up with my past duties while also taking on the responsibilities of my new position. As a result, I began rushing and introducing an error into the software code my team was updating.

The error led to a memory leak. We became aware of the issue when the performance was hindered, though we didn't immediately know the cause. I dove back into the code, reviewing recent changes, and ultimately determined the issue was a mistake on my end.

When I made that discovery, I took several steps. First, I let my team know that the error was mine and let them know its nature. Second, I worked with my team to correct the issue, resolving the memory leak.

Finally, I took this as a lesson about delegation. I began assigning work to my team more effectively, allowing me to excel as a manager and help them thrive as contributors. It was a crucial learning moment I have valued every day since.

Sample 3

If I identify a potential risk in a project, my first step is to assess the various factors that could lead to a poor outcome.

Prevention requires analysis. Ensuring I fully understand what can trigger the undesired event creates the proper foundation, allowing me to figure out how to reduce the likelihood of those events occurring.

Once I have the right understanding, I develop a mitigation plan. Precisely what this includes varies depending on the nature of the issue. However, it usually involves various steps and checks designed to monitor the project as it progresses to spot paths that may make the problem more likely to happen.

I find this approach effective as it combines knowledge and ongoing vigilance. If the project begins to head into risky territory, I can correct the trajectory.

Sample 4

This problem seems to occur every holiday season.

I've developed strategies to ensure that we have adequate staff coverage. The most crucial trick, I think, is to be proactive.

I keep a current list of personnel willing to come in at a moment's notice to fill others' shifts, especially around major holidays (when people are likely to call in sick). Each time an employee agrees to cover someone else's shift, I make a point to recognize them with a big thank you sign I write on our office whiteboard.

This keeps morale high enough that I can generally find someone to come in immediately. I also try to cross-train most of our staff so that they can cover for their colleagues when necessary. As a last resort, I'll protect their shift myself if required.

Sample 5

This happened nine months ago when our team was prepared to go live with a new product. A month before launch, we learned that one of our primary part's shipments would be delayed.

I immediately tried to contact with another supplier, and although I sourced one, they couldn't promise that they'd be able to deliver by our deadline. However, I was as transparent as possible throughout the situation, alerting management and our different department heads about the issue.

Fortunately, the R&D engineers were then able to do a quick redesign that allowed us to use another part we could access quickly, which turned out to be 20% cheaper than the original part!

We met our deadline and saved costs at the same time.

Sample 6

First, I analyze the situation rather than the employee's words to see what might have caused their discontent.

I would then speak with them privately, giving them a chance to air their grievance and myself the opportunity to work with them to find a solution.

Sometimes, all it takes to soothe employees is to let them know their opinions are respected. However, if the employee continued to spread negativity and diminish department morale,

I would put them on official notice to expect a formal performance review at the end of two weeks, at which point we would discuss their future with our department.

Sample 7

In my last job, I had a colleague who was consistently late for project meetings I was leading. At first, I tried a couple of gentle reminders of good practice/time-keeping when sending the agenda out for these weekly meetings.

After I found this was not working, I spoke to this colleague directly and asked him to join me for coffee at a nearby cafe. I broached the issue in a more casual environment, which took the pressure off, as colleagues didn't surround us. We had time to get to know each other a bit too.

I checked in to see if there was any particular reason for his repeated lateness, and it turned out that he had a regular meeting just before mine at a different worksite.

A quick fix was to move my meeting to a different day, which resolved the issue. Now I always check that new meetings I'm planning are held conveniently for all attendees.

Sample 8

I'm aware that every challenge will have its nuances. Rather than have a generic system, I like customizing my approach to match what has gone wrong.

For example, if an immediate solution is obvious and straightforward, I'll implement it without overthinking things. This happened recently when our IT system went down, and I quickly directed the interns to use phone lines to call our clients who were expecting deliveries that same day.

I can also assess and take time to fix unexpected problems requiring more finesse. There was a situation recently when one of our clients canceled a large order. I called meetings with the team and the client separately to determine what had gone wrong before offering a solution.

I'm glad it worked well, as the client returned on board.

"Little minds are tamed and subdued by misfortune, but great minds rise above it."

T 2 Tell Me A Time When You Led By Examples

Leading by example means guiding others through your behaviors and inspiring them to do the same. You provide a path to direct others down so everyone works toward a common goal with the same purpose. A leader makes it natural for people to want to do their best for their organization. You can accomplish this and have a workplace full of trust, confidence, and purpose.

Someone who leads by example can expect respect from their superiors, people who work alongside them, and their employees. Superiors see them as someone who can lead a team and inspire confidence in their work. Coworkers and employees see someone as having the ability to understand the workplace and how everyone works together truly. When you have the respect of the people you work with, you become a team on a joint mission.

Sample 1

In my current role, much foot traffic comes through the office. (Situation)

I manage the front desk, which means I am often the customers' first impression of the company. (Task)

I always choose to have a smile on my face, make eye contact, and show my excitement for the company for which I work. There are constant eyes on me, and I need to lead positively. (Action)

At least once per week, I receive comments regarding how impressed a customer was with my overall presence and attitude. (Result)

Sample 2

Last year our company merged with a competitor, and there was talk of pending layoffs. (Situation)

As the Sales Leader, my team closely monitors my actions. (Task)

I know that I must lead by example every moment of every day! Rather than show my stress, I encouraged my team to try harder than ever. I suggested that we show our corporate office precisely what we can do! (Action)

We ended up being the number one sales team in our region, which resulted in zero layoffs for our team. (Result)

Sample 3

In my current job, we have a lot of junior marketers on staff. (Situation)

As a more seasoned professional, I know these junior team members are impressionable. (Task)

I demonstrate leadership by always acting as though someone is watching. I behave how I want my team to behave and openly praise behavior that I want to see more of. I do much leading now by showcasing the proper approach in real-time rather than waiting for a formal meeting or performance review. (Action)

My philosophy has resulted in the rapid professional growth of these junior marketers. (Result)

Sample 4

I often lead by example, especially when it comes to mandatory overtime. (Situation)

I work in an order-driven environment, and sometimes we work late to finish the job. (Task)

Last week, we were asked to work overtime with just 5 hours notice. I did not let my peers see me get upset at the last-minute announcement. (Action)

As a result, we remained productive, and the mood remained upbeat. (Result)

Sample 5

My current company puts a lot of emphasis on accountability. (Situation)

Therefore, I purposefully lead by example in everything I do. (Task)

For instance, I strive to be early, arrive dressed for the part, and prepare for the next day before leaving the office. (Action)

As a result of my dedication and knack for leadership, I have received a few raises and title promotions over the years. (Result)

Sample 6

My students often come to class with their cell phones. They are scrolling through social media, answering texts, or allowing their phones to be a distraction at their desk. (Situation)

As their teacher and consistent influence, I attempt to lead through my actions. (Task)

I put my phone away and have a notebook and pen out instead. This way, it's clear that I'm on task. If I were on my phone, my students would not know if my actions were 100% work-related. (Action)

This example teaches my students to remain engaged and respectful of those around them. (Result)

Sample 7

While working for Company ABC, they announced closing their doors. (Situation)

I was the Plant Manager then, and all eyes were on me. (Task)

I chose never to display frustration, and I kept my poise. (Action)

As a result, I could retain 85% of my staff during the transition. I feel that my positive attitude helped others to feel hopeful. (Result)

Sample 8

We were working on a project requiring a lot of coordination and team management, but our supervisor fell sick at the last moment, and we were all confused about our next step.

In that time of confusion, I took the lead and managed the whole project until the supervisor returned. He was very happy with my work.

"Motivation is what gets you started. Habit is what keeps you going."

U 1 Give An Example of When You Performed Well Under Pressure and How Do You Handle It?

You're guaranteed to get asked this question in any high-stress work environment.

Sample 1

I perform a lot better when under a lot of pressure. The sense of urgency and importance motivates me to up my game and make sure everything works out right.

When I worked as a Financial Analyst at XYZ Inc., most of the work was very high pressure. I had to go above and beyond the line of duty to ensure we met the tight deadlines set by our clients. This often meant working 12-hour work days and sometimes over the weekend.

Sample 2

As a seasonal worker, my entire career has been high-pressure. My last position was as a line cook at the Peter Cat Restaurant in Kolkata during the summer.

Around 3 out of 4 months were high-stress, there was a lot of work, and the restaurant was always full. I've even had to skip breaks to ensure we weren't understaffed.

Sample 3

As an entry-level marketer, there was not much expected of me at NICCO Inc. My main to-dos involved doing research and completing whatever tasks were assigned to me.

I devised an excellent idea to market the company during a content marketing brainstorming session. The gist was to interview company clients who successfully used the software, create case studies on what they're doing, and include it in our email marketing strategy.

Sample 4

I'm not someone who is energized by or succeeds in stressful environments. My first step in managing stress is to get around it by keeping my work processes organized and my attitude professional.

When customers or associates come to me with issues, I look at things from their perspective and initiate a collaborative problem-solving approach to keep the situation from escalating.

Maintaining an efficient, congenial office with open lines of communication automatically reduces workplace stress. Of course, sometimes unexpected stressors will arise. When this happens, I take a deep breath, remembering that the person I'm dealing with is frustrated with a situation, not with me. I then actively listen to their concerns and make a plan to resolve the issue as quickly as possible.

But it's important not to dismiss stress (i.e., don't say, I just put my head down and push through it, or I don't get stressed out). Instead, please talk about your go-to strategies for dealing with stress (whether it's meditating for 10 minutes every day, making sure you go for a run, or keeping a super-detailed to-do list) and how you communicate and otherwise proactively try to lessen pressure.

Sample 5

I deal with pressure or stressful situations by reminding myself that things are temporary and ensuring I stay grounded and understand what I can and cannot change. I know when and how to ask for help from my team members or manager and take things one step at a time.

This is a chance to demonstrate your ability to stay calm and work through any challenging situation and your emotional intelligence.

Sample 6

No matter how much one tries, with the job scenes getting more demanding, one feels stressed at some point.

Over the years, I have learned to transform all the stress into efficient performance. At my previous job, I remember that the stress of giving my best in every project drove me to complete the tasks well in advance.

To balance things out, I also regularly involve myself in outdoor activities like tennis and badminton to be mentally and physically fit to handle any pressure.

Sample 7

Though I can't particularly say I enjoy stressful situations, I am very good at working under pressure. I tend to step back, think, plan, and prioritize during chaos and panic.

For example, there have been times I've had to juggle multiple university projects and assignments simultaneously. I would divide large assignments into small, individual tasks and prioritize them.

Sample 8

I prefer working under pressure. It is a challenge where I must up my game to succeed.

Working under pressure is pretty much part of the job as a cook. I've been in several situations where the restaurant was understaffed for the occasion. It's pretty much a constant thing during peak season.

When many orders are coming in, and we can barely keep up, I tend to get significantly more productive than usual.

You measure the size of the accomplishment by the obstacles you had to overcome to reach your goals.

"Ambition is the path to success. Persistence is the vehicle you arrive in."

U 2 Describe A Situation In Which You Were Able To Use Persuasion To Convince Someone Successfully.

Sample 1

In my last job as a warehouse supervisor, I tried to convince the logistics manager to change the organization of the entire warehouse. I proposed a concept to them, but they were stubborn and considered the existing system effective enough. I did not give up, though. Preparing a visualization on my laptop and doing some calculations and forecasts, I showed them exactly, in numbers, how much we could shorten the expedition time with the new model. Finally, they were convinced, and we got a green light. The logistics manager was rational, and they changed their mind when they saw the numbers.

Sample 2

I led a group of manual workers in a small production plant, and we had a random audit announced the next day. It was something unprecedented in the company. We needed everyone to stay overtime, work until 10 pm, or even longer. But workers did not want to stay. They were tired, had other plans, and weren't loyal to their employer. I couldn't convince them with words or promises of a bonus, so I opted for emotions. It was the only time that I cried at work. But something within them changed when they saw a seemingly untouchable manager falling into tears right before them. Maybe they saw something human in my behavior, or perhaps it helped them understand the situation's seriousness. I cannot say. But they agreed to stay overtime, and we prepared the place for the audit.

Sample 3

This is my first job application, and I don't have a similar experience at work. However, I can refer to my personal life. My younger sister didn't want to attend college. She had her crisis of adolescence and wanted to pursue higher ideals as an activist. My parents could not convince her with their arguments. Then I intervened. What I did was that I tried to explain to her how the college could help her in her career as an activist. I explained the powerful connections she would make while studying at college, the people she would meet and make interested in her projects, and how the general public would perceive her with different eyes once she had a degree. Instead of trying to convince her to follow a path of an employee and earn good money, which was my parents' strategy, I showed her how college studies would help her achieve the goals she wanted to achieve. It worked, and she enrolled in college.

Sample 4

In my last job in sales, I tried to acquire a big customer. They didn't respond positively to my emails or calls. But I continued to send them more offers relevant to their business. I even sent the manager a greeting card with a small present when they had a birthday. I was persistent in trying to build a relationship with them. When they finally needed a significant upgrade to their ERP system, guess who they contacted first? They got me, and we eventually closed the deal.

Sample 5

In my last teaching job, I struggled with a student. They came from a difficult background. Broken family, bad role models, criminal friends, you name it. They suffered because of their past and caused problems in each of my lessons. But I did not give up on them. Oppositely, I gave them a lot of attention. That's what they were seeking, attention and understanding. I had several one on one meetings with them. Instead of trying to convince them with disciplinary measures, I used empathy and positive encouragement. Eventually, they improved their behavior, at least somehow. I persuaded them to act better in my classes, though other teachers still struggled with their behavior.

Sample 6

My biggest battle was to persuade myself to have confidence in my abilities. I've had my share of problems, and most people around me told me I was no good for anything. My confidence suffered, and I was timid in relationships. But I decided I had to change things. I took the initiative, read motivational books, visited a psychologist, and joined a sports club to learn to interact with people again. All of this happened three years ago, and now, looking back, I can hardly recognize my old self. I succeeded in persuading myself of my worth. If I failed, I would not sit here today with you, interviewing for a great job.

Sample 7

My last job was all about persuasion. We were selling a promise, a dream, rather than a product. That's how it works with risky investment opportunities, and as an account executive in a brokerage firm, my job was to sell such opportunities. I always tried to explain to the prospect the vision of their future and how something they do today can change the life they will live in ten years. It was a lot about visualization and deducing what they may dream about, whether they were a family person or had some other dreams. As an account executive, I did not fare badly and convinced many clients. But now I am looking for a different job.

"It is better to fail in originality than to succeed in imitation."

V 1 What Have You Learned From Your Mistakes?

The best way to answer this question is to talk about a specific example of a time you made a mistake. Briefly explain what the mistake was, but don't dwell on it. Quickly switch to what you learned or how you improved after making that mistake. You might also explain the steps you took to ensure that mistake never happened again.

It's also a good idea to mention something relatively minor. Avoid mentioning any mistakes that demonstrate a flaw in your character (for example, when you got in trouble for fighting at work).

Sometimes a good mistake to mention is a team mistake. You don't want to place all the blame on your teammates, but you can say that you collectively made an error.

Sample 1

When I started working as a project manager, I made a mistake that ended up causing some delays in the project. I had misunderstood a communication from the client, so we had to redo some work. This caused my team some frustration and extra work, and the project was delayed by a week.

However, I learned a lot from this mistake. First of all, I learned the importance of clear communication. From then on, I made sure to clarify any communication that I received from the client, and I also made sure to communicate clearly with my team. This helped to prevent any misunderstandings in the future.

I realized that it's important to be proactive when preventing mistakes. I started implementing more thorough checks and balances throughout the project to ensure everything was on track. I also involved my team members in these processes so everyone knew what was happening and could help catch any mistakes.

Overall, I think this mistake was a valuable learning experience for me. It helped me to become a more effective project manager, and it also helped me to develop better communication and problem-solving skills.

Sample 2

In addition to learning the importance of maintaining a schedule and managing appointments, I also learned the value of clear communication. After the double-booking incident, I realized that it was essential to communicate any changes or conflicts in schedules with clients and executives in a timely manner. This helped to prevent any misunderstandings or conflicts from arising.

Furthermore, the experience taught me the importance of staying calm and composed in high-pressure situations. I had to assess the situation quickly, acknowledge the client's frustration, and work to find a solution that would satisfy everyone involved. This experience helped me develop my problem-solving skills and gave me the confidence to handle similar situations.

My mistake as a receptionist taught me a lot about the importance of effective communication, time management, and staying calm under pressure. I continue to use these valuable skills in my current role, and will serve me well in future positions.

Sample 3

When I started as an assistant manager of a sales branch, I was eager to prove myself and take on all the responsibilities. However, I soon realized that working that way was not sustainable or effective. I found myself getting burnt out and unable to prioritize tasks effectively.

After self-reflection and observing the successful managers around me, I learned the importance of delegating tasks to the appropriate team members. By delegating tasks, I could focus on the bigger picture and ensure everything ran smoothly. This also allowed me to identify areas where my team members needed support and provide appropriate training or resources.

Through this experience, I also discovered that effective delegation involves understanding the strengths and weaknesses of each team member and assigning tasks accordingly. This approach helped me accomplish more as a manager, empowered my team members, and helped them develop new skills and confidence.

Since then, I have implemented this delegation strategy in my management roles and have seen great success. I have won several awards for my management skills, and I believe my ability to delegate effectively has played a significant role in achieving those accolades. I am confident I can bring this experience and expertise to any new position and contribute to the team's success.

Sample 4

Last year, I was tapped to present to the company's finance team to make a case for adding funds to my team's budget to revamp the company's online store. The presentation landed during our busiest time of year, and I was swamped. Because I was overwhelmed, I convinced myself I knew the information and didn't need to prepare for the presentation. In short, I blew it. We didn't get the money we needed, and I disappointed my team.

This happened because I was overly confident and didn't set my priorities well. Since then, I've always found time to prepare for presentations, even if it means taking the material home to practice. My presentations have brought in some of the biggest deals our company has seen this past year since the mistake, so I used that failure as a learning experience and a chance to improve myself.

Sample 5

Thank you for asking about what I've learned from my mistakes. One of the most valuable lessons I've learned is the importance of persistence. I used to give up easily when faced with a challenge, but now I understand that the solution is often right in front of me if I keep pushing forward. Another lesson I've learned is the importance of not judging people based on first impressions. I've found that giving every person a second chance can lead to unexpected positive outcomes. Finally, I used to think there was only one correct answer to a problem, but I've learned that thinking creatively and considering different perspectives can lead to even better solutions. I believe that everyone makes mistakes, and the important thing is to learn from them and grow as a person and professional. If you would like me to provide an example of a mistake I've learned from, I would be happy to share an experience from my previous position that isn't directly related to the requirements of this job.

Sample 6

One important lesson that I have learned from my past mistakes is the value of asking for help. I understand it is much better to ask for clarification and resolve an issue immediately rather than tackle a problem on my own and potentially worsen it. Through my experiences, I have learned that there is no shame in asking for help when needed and that it can be a sign of strength and initiative.

My willingness to ask questions and seek guidance from others would be a great fit for your company's emphasis on teamwork and open communication. I am confident in my ability to collaborate effectively with my colleagues, and I recognize the importance of working together to achieve shared goals.

My experience recognizing the importance of asking for help has helped me develop greater self-awareness and humility. I understand that I don't know everything and that there is always room for improvement and growth. I can learn and improve more quickly and effectively by seeking feedback and guidance from others.

Sample 6

I genuinely believe that making mistakes is an opportunity for growth and improvement. A few years ago, I was part of a team that failed to land a major sale, and it was a real wake-up call for me. Our visuals were identified as one of the key issues, and I took it upon myself to learn as much as possible about creating effective visual presentations.

Over the next six months, I spent much of my free time learning how to use various software programs to create more engaging and persuasive visuals. I took online courses, read books, and practiced until I felt confident in my abilities. And since then, I've been continuously praised for my visuals in meetings and sales pitches.

I learned from that experience that investing time and effort into improving my skills pays off in the long run. I also learned that it's important to be proactive in seeking feedback and identifying areas for improvement. I'm excited to bring this attitude and dedication to continuous learning to any role I take on in the future.

"Don't raise your voice. Improve your argument."

V 2 Describe What You Did During the Gap or Why There is a Gap Between Your Employment

You took time off to complete your MBA, prepared for and passed the Certified Financial Planner designation test, focused on some volunteer work, and started a new mentoring program for inner-city youth. These are all answers that emphasize your time off's positive aspects. It's important to share any skills or knowledge you cultivated during your time off, especially if you developed a new skill to increase your relevance in the workforce or worked in some other productive way.

You might want to share that story if you took time off to address a personal concern and resolve the issue. For example, you could mention taking time off to rehabilitate from an injury or help care for an elderly parent. The key is to describe the issue as a past problem that will no longer interfere with productivity.

You took time off to do something fun, like spending the winter skiing, traveling through Europe, or mastering golf. It's important to demonstrate that you had a solid work ethic before and after your break. You should provide examples of how hard you worked on key projects before and after your break and offer recommendations from supervisors who can attest to your long hours, high energy, and optimal investment in the job.

You were laid off from a job resulting in a period of unemployment. Share the reasons why there was a reduction in the workforce and reference any indicators that you were in good standing at the time. If the gaps in your resume are a product of termination, you need to prove to your employer that the reasons you were fired no longer affect your overall performance. For example, I was a principal then and had difficulty managing the budget effectively. I decided to return to my first love, teaching, where I had previously excelled, and you can see that my teaching reviews have been very positive since then.

Regardless of the reason for your gap in employment, it's essential to focus on your accomplishments. Share as much concrete evidence of your success in the jobs before the gap and after you resumed employment, itemizing your accomplishments by referring to situations where you intervened, specific actions you took, and the results you generated. Emphasize how your company benefited from your role, and demonstrate your continued commitment to your work.

Sample 1

Taking a break from the traditional office setting allowed me to focus on my daughter's arrival and spend quality time with her during her early years. At the same time, I wanted to keep my legal skills up to date, so I volunteered my time one day a week at a nonprofit organization. It was a rewarding experience, allowing me to give back to the community while keeping my legal skills sharp.

Now that my daughter is in preschool, I'm excited to return to the workplace and apply the knowledge and skills I've gained during my break. I'm confident that my experience as a mother has taught me valuable skills such as patience, multitasking, and time management, which I believe are transferable to any work environment. I'm eager to join a team where I can contribute my legal expertise and learn from others.

I understand there may be some concerns about my employment gap. Still, I hope my dedication to pro bono work demonstrates my commitment to the legal field and my willingness to stay involved even when not working in a traditional office environment. I'm eager to discuss how my skills and experiences can benefit your company and contribute to its success.

Sample 2

Since you're in the publishing industry, you likely heard about the layoffs at XYZ company. After being part of those layoffs, I wanted to assess my next steps carefully. Although it was a difficult time, I saw it as an opportunity to reevaluate my career goals and develop new skills. I took several classes to sharpen my marketing-related skills and learn about emerging trends in the industry. These classes have been instrumental in helping me understand the latest marketing strategies and techniques that are relevant to the publishing industry.

I am excited to transition into a new role and apply my skills and knowledge in a new environment. I am particularly interested in the position at ABC company because of the company's reputation for innovation and creativity. I believe that my experience, combined with my newly developed skills, make me an excellent fit for the marketing team at ABC.

I look forward to contributing to the company's success and learning from the talented professionals on the team.

Sample 3

My last position didn't align with my skill set, and performing some required tasks was challenging. Ultimately, my position was terminated, which was a humbling experience. However, I saw this as an opportunity to grow and learn from the experience. I reflected on how I handled the situation and what I could have done differently. As a result, I learned the importance of asking for help and continuing my education and training.

Since then, I've taken several classes and worked with a career coach to improve my skills and better understand the industry. This has allowed me to develop new skills and broaden my perspective, which I believe will be valuable in a new role.

I am excited about the opportunity to bring my renewed enthusiasm and skills to a new position, such as this one at your company. I am confident that my lessons will make me a better employee, and I am eager to apply them positively and productively.

Sample 4

Unfortunately, I had to quit my job due to an accident during that period. It was a challenging phase as I have always been highly active, constantly using my cognitive abilities to innovate and excel in my work. However, I also learned a lot from that experience. It made me realize my extreme passion for my work, and I knew that at least no accident could stop me from being mentally active.

I started reading books and keeping tabs on the latest technologies to keep my mind engaged and stay in touch with the latest advancements in my field. This allowed me to stay updated and maintain my knowledge base, despite being away from the workplace. Moreover, during my recovery, I also volunteered at a local nonprofit organization, which helped me gain a fresh perspective on using my skills to impact the community positively.

Overall, while the accident was a setback, it allowed me to take a step back and reassess my priorities. It also helped me develop resilience and adaptability, skills I believe will be valuable assets in any work environment. I am eager to apply my renewed energy and passion to a new role and continue growing personally and professionally.

Sample 5

For the past six months, I have taken a break from work to focus on traveling and spending quality time with my children. It has been a wonderful experience, and I feel grateful for this opportunity. However, after being laid off in May, I realized I needed to start looking for work again. I postponed my job search until after my kids returned to school from their summer vacation. During this time, we had the chance to travel to Srinagar, which was an incredible experience. We explored new places, tried fresh foods, and made unforgettable memories.

In August, I began my job search with renewed focus and enthusiasm. I am excited to find a new opportunity to use my skills and experience to make a meaningful contribution. My time off has given me a fresh perspective, and I am eager to bring this to my next role. I also understand that employment gaps can sometimes raise concerns for employers, so I am transparent about my situation and have included only the years of my employment history in my resume.

"Optimism is the one quality more associated with success and happiness than any other."

W 1 Are You Willing To Travel, Or How Much Are You Willing To Travel?

The hiring manager may also come out and tell you how much travel is involved and then ask an interview question to determine if this is an acceptable travel amount. In this case, you can indicate that you are on board with their proposal if acceptable. For example, you could say:

That amount of travel will work for me. I traveled that same amount in my last company, and it worked fine.

It's always good to show you've done something successfully in the past. This is the best way to prove to a new employer that you'll be successful for them too!

Another thing to keep in mind is the actual travel schedule. Two jobs could have the same travel percentage say 50%. But one could have you spending two weeks away and then two weeks at home, while the other could have you traveling for 2-3 days at a time, returning, and doing it all again a few days later.

Depending on your family, children, etc., you may be able to handle one of these travel requirements but not the other. So the travel duration and schedule are other things you should clarify before answering. You can say, I want to understand the company travel schedule better. Can you give me an example of how long each trip would be or what a typical month looks like? This will help you get a clear picture of what your work schedule would look like before you answer the interview question.

If you're interested in the job but can't travel quite as much as they're proposing, you can say:

I don't think I can travel quite that amount. The job and work sound interesting, and I'd love to consider the position if the travel requirements can be reduced to 30 percent.

This may or may not work (it depends on the role and the company's flexibility), but it's worth asking! This way, you'll find out the best they can do! You're not accepting the job or signing a contract. You're just indicating whether this might be possible for you.

Sample 1

Traveling for work is a new experience, but I will take on the challenge. Although I do not know what to expect, I am willing to learn and adapt to the job's demands. I understand that traveling may impact my schedule and personal life, but I am ready to make the necessary adjustments to succeed in this role.

I am excited about the opportunity to learn new things and gain new experiences through travel. Exposure to different cultures and environments can broaden my perspective and make me a well-rounded individual. I am also eager to meet new people and develop professional relationships that benefit the company.

While stepping out of my comfort zone can be daunting, I am confident that I have the skills and determination to overcome any challenges that may arise during business travel. I am committed to being a valuable asset to the company and believe that traveling can help me achieve this goal.

Sample 2

In my previous role as a sales representative, I was on the road for half of my working hours, traveling to different states to meet with clients and attend trade shows. I developed strong time management skills and became comfortable with frequent travel. I enjoyed the new experiences and challenges of being on the go.

When I saw this job description, and it required only 25% travel time, I felt it was an excellent fit for me. I am more than willing to travel for this company when needed, whether to attend conferences or visit clients in other cities. I understand that travel can be demanding and tiring, but I'm confident that my previous experience has prepared me well.

Sample 3

I'm being candid, and I must say that if I had a choice, I would prefer not to travel. As a parent of two children, I understand the value of spending quality time with family and like to stay in the city during the week. However, I also recognize that every job has its own set of challenges and downsides. That being said, I like everything about this position – my duties, responsibilities, the team, the company culture, and the potential to achieve great things here. I'm eager to learn new skills and take on new challenges, and I believe that this job will provide me with ample opportunities to do so.

I understand that to get the most out of this job. I will need to make some sacrifices. While traveling may not be my first choice, I am willing to do it if I can be a part of this team and contribute to its success. I'm confident that the travel required will be reasonable, and I'm prepared to handle it as efficiently and effectively as possible.

Sample 4

Yes, I'm willing to travel. I see business trips as an opportunity to broaden my horizons and gain valuable industry insights. Attending conferences, training, and other events is crucial to keeping up with the latest trends and technologies, and I always take full advantage of these opportunities.

I understand that travel may be necessary to help the company succeed, and I'm committed to doing whatever it takes to contribute to that success. Whether meeting with clients or partners, conducting site visits, or attending trade shows, I'm always travel game.

I'm highly adaptable and can easily work independently or as part of a team while on the road. I'm comfortable with making travel arrangements and handling any unexpected situations that may arise. My willingness to travel and ability to adapt to new situations make me a valuable asset to any company.

Sample 5

As someone with five years of production management experience, I have grown accustomed to traveling. For instance, I flew to China twice a year in my previous role to ensure our factories were operating effectively. I made meaningful connections with our Chinese employees during these business trips. I even attended the Beijing Summer Olympics, one of my favorite memories.

Sample 6

I read the job description carefully and know that regular business travels are part of this job. But I am willing and even eager to travel. It was one of the reasons why I applied for a job with you. I enjoy traveling, meeting people from different cultures, and learning new things. And since I don't have a family, nothing is holding me back.

Sample 7

I am open to travel if it doesn't interfere with my studies. I understand the importance of balancing work and education, and I am committed to completing my studies and being a dedicated employee. However, I would be available to travel on the occasional weekend or make trips that only last a day, as this would not significantly impact my studies.

Travel is an exciting experience, and I am always eager to learn and explore new places. As a student, my schedule can be flexible during specific periods, such as winter and summer breaks. I am happy to take advantage of these opportunities to travel for work. Your next conference is during my winter break, so I would be free to attend this trip.

I believe that travel can be a valuable part of professional growth and development, and I am open to going on as many trips as my schedule as a student allows. I would happily travel and represent the company if I could balance my work responsibilities and academic commitments.

Sample 8

I firmly believe that in-person meetings are essential for building strong business relationships. However, I am also conscious of the impact of travel on the environment. Therefore, I would be willing to travel when necessary, but I also believe we should try to balance in-person and online meetings. Technology has made it easier to communicate with our business partners remotely, and we should take advantage of this whenever possible. That being said, I understand that meeting in person is sometimes necessary to build trust and strengthen relationships.

Regarding travel, I am always mindful of my carbon footprint. I try to reduce my impact on the environment by using public transportation whenever possible and staying in eco-friendly hotels. I also make an effort to pack light and avoid unnecessary waste.

I believe that we can find a balance between face-to-face meetings and online communication while also being mindful of the impact of travel on the environment. I am willing to travel when necessary, but I also believe we should consider alternatives whenever possible.

Sample 9

Traveling for work would be an amazing opportunity to see new places, meet new people, and gain new experiences. In my opinion, the ability to travel is a valuable aspect of any job, as it allows you to see the world and better understand different cultures and ways of life.

As a sales representative, I had the opportunity to travel frequently and found it incredibly rewarding. I met with clients face-to-face and established stronger connections, increasing sales and revenue for the company. Additionally, I learned about different business practices and customs that I could bring back and implement in our company through travel.

I'm excited about the prospect of traveling for this job and look forward to the many opportunities it will provide for personal and professional growth.

"Believe you can, and you're halfway there."

W 2 Why Have You Switched Jobs So Many Times?

As for why you have switched jobs so many times, it's important to address any concerns the interviewer may have. Job-hopping can be seen as a red flag for HR managers, so it's essential to communicate your reasons for switching jobs. Possibly you had a valid reason for leaving a job after a short period, such as the company culture not being a good fit for you.

However, some companies may be skeptical and assume you're a job hopper always looking for a better salary offer. Others may think you're unqualified for the job and quit because you couldn't deliver, or you get bored quickly and quit. Your goal is to convince the interviewer that you don't fall into any of these categories and are committed to staying with the company long-term.

One way to answer this question is to explain why you switched jobs. Perhaps the company culture wasn't a good fit for you, or the job description was misleading, and you ended up doing something you either didn't enjoy or weren't qualified for. Alternatively, you may have learned that you didn't enjoy the job and weren't willing to continue doing something that didn't bring you fulfillment. While this may not be the ideal answer, being honest and upfront with the interviewer about your reasons for leaving previous positions is important.

Sample 1

Taking up challenging assignments has always been my forte. It not only helps me expand my skill set but also enables me to think outside the box and develop innovative solutions. Client satisfaction and manager appreciation are the best rewards for a well-done job. It motivates me to push my limits and strive for excellence in everything I do.

The opportunity to work as a sales manager in your esteemed organization is something I am excited about. I have always been passionate about sales and the thrill of closing deals. It will be a great opportunity to sell products I am genuinely interested in and believe in.

Apart from the satisfaction of doing a good job, achieving my financial goals is also important. Working as a sales manager will allow me to do just that. I am confident I can achieve my targets and exceed expectations in this role.

I am eager to take on this role and contribute to the success of your organization. My passion, drive, and determination will make me an asset to your team, and I am excited to participate.

Sample 2

Well, to start with, my first job after graduating from university was in a big corporation, where I learned a lot about software engineering practices. However, I also discovered that working in a company with many regulations and rules was not the right fit for me. So, at the end of my internship there, I decided to try my hand at working for a startup. I enjoyed that job significantly more as it allowed me to solve problems creatively without being told how to do them. Unfortunately, the startup failed to raise money and went out of business, putting me back on the job market.

After exploring different options, I came across Asian Paints, the company I have always wanted to work for. I have heard much about your company's culture and values and believe I would fit in perfectly. I am excited about possibly working for your organization and contributing to its success.

Sample 3

I have been fortunate to work for my present company and have been allowed to develop several professional skills, including interpersonal and managerial skills. However, I have recently realized that my true calling is in a different sector where I can make a more significant social impact. I am passionate about using my skills to help others and strongly believe in giving back to the community. This is why I am particularly drawn to your company, which aims to serve underprivileged children. I would be honored to be a part of an organization committed to making a positive difference in the lives of those in need. I am excited about the possibility of contributing my skills and experience to your team and helping to further your mission.

Sample 4

I was disappointed with the role as it did not align with my interests and skillet. Despite my efforts to communicate my concerns to my manager, they could not offer me the kind of work I was passionate about. As a result, I felt unfulfilled and not challenged in my role. This experience taught me the importance of clear communication and alignment between the job description and responsibilities. I realized that I need to work in an environment where I can utilize my strengths and passions to make a meaningful impact. That's why I am excited about the opportunity to work with your company, where I believe my skills and interests align with your mission and vision. I can contribute positively to your team and help achieve your goals.

Sample 5

You may label me a frequent career-changer, but my experiences have made me a far better employee today. My past job switches have helped me develop better interpersonal skills, gain diverse experiences, and adapt to rapidly changing business environments,

As a result, I can now solve problems more efficiently and creatively, as I have learned to thrive in ambiguous and uncertain situations. My first job taught me patience, while my second job helped me master spreadsheets and data analysis. My third job allowed me to develop better people skills and adapt to working with culturally diverse and geographically dispersed teams.

I am confident that my varied background makes me an ideal candidate for this job role today.

Sample 6

Working with multiple companies in a short period was not what I had planned for my career. However, looking back, it has been an enriching journey. Each company had unique challenges and opportunities, which helped me develop diverse skills and experiences.

Although one of the companies was going through a rough patch, it taught me the importance of resilience and perseverance. I learned how to work under pressure and stay motivated during difficult times.

As a result of my experiences, I am now confident in my ability to adapt to new situations and find ways to make a positive impact. I believe that this versatility and adaptability will serve me well in any future roles.

I seek stability and a long-term career with a reputable organization like yours. I want to work with a company that shares my values and provides me with opportunities for growth and development. I believe that a longer stint with a single company will enable me to deepen my knowledge and expertise and contribute meaningfully to the organization.

Sample 7

I never expected to work with so many companies in these few years. The companies I worked for were small; one was even going through a terrible patch.

But honestly, my journey has been a rewarding one. I can now confidently walk into a new situation and figure out ways to make a difference. This was meant to happen, and I wouldn't exchange all the experience I've gained from my switches for anything!

But I am seriously looking forward to not having to do this anymore soon. I want to do a stint lasting 5 to 10 years with a reputed organization such as yours. This will make my career stable and fruitful in the long run.

Sample 8

Over the past five years, I've been extremely fortunate to have been presented with some fantastic opportunities in my career. It all started with my time at FedEx, where I spent three years honing my skills and developing professionally. My experience during this time was invaluable and prepared me for the next step in my career.

That next step came when I was recruited for a fantastic management opportunity at Amazon. I spent a year and a half there, learning about cutting-edge technologies and working alongside some of the brightest minds in the industry. It was a tremendous learning experience, and I felt like I had grown leaps and bounds there.

But then, something unexpected happened. My former manager at FedEx reached out to me with an opportunity at Uber. It was a senior position with much more responsibility, and I knew it was an opportunity

I couldn't pass up. Even though I wasn't actively looking for a job, I knew this was a chance to take my career to the next level.

These opportunities have given me a wealth of experience and skills that will be invaluable as I advance in my career. I'm excited to see where this journey takes me. Still, I'm also looking forward to finding a stable position to make a long-term impact and grow alongside a reputable organization.

"Happiness is not by chance, but by choice. I never dreamed about success. I worked for it."

X 1 Are You Willing To Relocate?

I am incredibly excited about joining your team and contributing my skills and experience to your company's success. The job description aligns perfectly with my career goals, and I believe my background and expertise make me an ideal fit for this role.

While I am not currently in a position to relocate, I am committed to exploring all possible options and finding creative solutions to ensure I can fully commit myself to this job. If the company is willing to work with me on a flexible work arrangement, I am confident I can make a meaningful contribution from a distance. However, if the job requires me to relocate, I am open to discussing the possibilities and determining the best course of action.

I am passionate about this job and am committed to doing whatever it takes to make it work. My skills, experience, and enthusiasm make me the perfect fit for this position, and I am excited about the opportunity to join your team and make a difference.

Sample 1

I am very passionate about my city and quite content with living here. If the job opportunity requires me to relocate within this city, I would have no problem doing so. I am familiar with the city's culture and lifestyle and have established a network of friends and acquaintances. It would be relatively easy to transition within the city, and I would be excited to explore new neighborhoods and experiences.

However, I am still open if the position requires relocation to a different city. It would be a great chance to broaden my horizons, meet new people, and learn about different cultures. I enjoy traveling and exploring new places, and relocating to a new city would give me a fresh perspective and a chance to expand my knowledge and understanding of the world.

While relocating to a different city may present challenges, such as finding a new place to live, adjusting to a new environment, and building a new social network, I am up for the challenge. I am a quick learner and adaptable, and I am confident that I can adjust to any new situation that comes my way.

While I am pretty happy living in my current city, I am open to relocating for the right job opportunity. I am excited about the prospect of learning about new people, places, and cultures and am ready to embrace any challenges that come my way.

Demonstrating your high level of interest in the position is essential. Remember that the recruiter may ask about your willingness to relocate to gauge your commitment to the job. While discussing relocation is essential, the job should remain your primary focus.

Make sure to communicate what you're looking for in the company. Both you and the recruiter have expectations, so discuss your role, growth opportunities, expectations for you, and any other relevant factors. Gaining clarity about the job can help you make an informed decision about relocation.

Regardless of your relocation decision, express your strong interest in working with the company. This is a crucial point to convey during the interview.

This common interview question can generally be categorized into three responses: Yes, Maybe, and No. Here are some sample answers for each option.

If the interviewer asks if you're open to relocation, and your answer is "Yes," you can respond with something like.

Sample 2

Yes, I am open to relocation. As a recent graduate, I'm eager to take on new challenges and gain exposure to different environments. I believe the job profile offered by your company would give me an incredible opportunity to learn and grow in my career. Relocating for such a fantastic opportunity would be an easy decision for me.

I'm excited about exploring a new city, meeting new people, and experiencing a different way of life. I can adapt to any new environment and thrive in a new workplace. The chance to work for a company with a strong reputation and to build my skills and knowledge is very important to me.

If the job requires me to relocate, I am ready and willing to take on that challenge. Moving to a new place can be difficult, but I am fully prepared to handle any logistics involved and make a smooth transition. I am committed to the job and the company, and relocating would be a great way to demonstrate that commitment.

In summary, expressing your openness to relocation demonstrates your willingness to embrace new opportunities and enthusiasm for the job. It also shows the interviewer that you are adaptable and committed to the company's goals.

Sample 3

I am open to the option of relocation for the right opportunity. In this case, I am very excited about the job profile offered by your company and the potential for growth and development within the organization. The opportunity to learn and advance my career is incredibly important to me, and I believe that your company provides the perfect platform for achieving these goals.

I also want to emphasize that I am confident that my previous years of experience will be a valuable asset to your organization. I am eager to bring my skills and knowledge to the table and contribute to the company's success in any way possible.

I am relocating and understand that moving to a new place can be challenging, but I am willing to take on that challenge for this job. I am excited about exploring a new city and meeting new people. I am also confident I can adapt to any new environment and thrive in a new workplace.

I am fully committed to this job and your company's success. Relocating for this opportunity would be a decision I would make with enthusiasm and excitement. Thank you for considering me for this role, and I look forward to the opportunity to contribute to your organization meaningfully.

By expressing your willingness to relocate, you demonstrate to the interviewer that you are committed to the job and the company and willing to take on new challenges to further your career growth. This enthusiasm and commitment can help you stand out from other candidates who may be less inclined to relocate

If the answer to the question "Are you willing to relocate?" is "Maybe," you could respond in the following manner.

Sample 4

I am open to the possibility of relocation, but I would need to consider the details of the opportunity and how it would fit with my circumstances. I have certain family and personal commitments that I need to consider before deciding about relocating.

I am interested in this job and could contribute to your company. I would be willing to explore the possibility of relocation if the job offers great learning opportunities and potential for growth within the company. If the job aligns with my personal and professional goals, I would be happy to discuss relocation further and explore options that could work for both parties.

However, I need more information about the relocation requirements and limitations and any support your company could offer to make the transition easier for me and my family. This includes relocation expenses, temporary housing, and other logistical arrangements.

I am interested in exploring this opportunity further and would be open to relocating if it aligns with my personal and professional goals. I appreciate your understanding and flexibility as we discuss this further.

Expressing your willingness to consider relocation, you show that you are open-minded and willing to consider all options. However, by being transparent about your circumstances and asking for more information, you can decide whether relocation is viable. This honesty and transparency can help build trust with the interviewer and demonstrate your professionalism.

Sample 5

I appreciate the opportunity you have presented and am excited about the job role you offer. However, I have recently started a family, and relocating to a new city is a significant decision that requires careful consideration.

Before I make any commitments, I would like to take some time to discuss this matter with my partner and family to determine if relocating is a feasible option for us. Can you please provide me with more details about the relocation requirements and limitations, such as any relocation packages or support the company offers? This information would be helpful in my decision-making process.

I understand this may require some time, but I want to make the best decision for my family and career. Can I get back to you within a week with a decision?

I want to reiterate that I am highly interested in this job role and the potential growth opportunities within your company. I believe my skills and experience would make a valuable contribution to your team. I hope you can appreciate my position and understand that this decision is significant for me and my family.

I appreciate your understanding and look forward to discussing this further with you.

By expressing your need for time to consider the decision and asking for more information about relocation packages, you show that you are thoughtful and considerate of your personal and professional commitments. This approach demonstrates your professionalism and interest in the job while ensuring you make an informed decision that works best for you and your family.

If the answer is No, it is important to convey your interest in the job role and your willingness to consider relocating if circumstances permit.

However, if relocating is not an option, expressing your desire to work remotely and still be a part of the organization is important. Here is an example response.

Sample 6

While I appreciate the opportunity and am impressed with the job role offered by your company, I am not in a position to relocate. I have just moved to (city's name) and settling in. However, I would like to express my interest in the job, and I am willing to work remotely if the opportunity presents itself. I can add value to your organization through my skills and experience. If remote work is an option, I would happily explore that possibility. I am confident that we can develop a mutually beneficial arrangement that works for both of us.

In this way, you can convey your interest in the job and desire to work with the company while being honest about your current situation and preferences. This approach shows that you are flexible, adaptable, and willing to explore different options to make the job work for you and the company.

Sample 7

I appreciate the opportunity that your company is offering me. However, I am currently settled in this city with my family and have no plans to relocate. I am genuinely passionate about this industry and would like to explore other opportunities available in my current location. If your company has any other positions that match my skills and experience, I would like to discuss those opportunities further.

By expressing your appreciation for the opportunity and your willingness to explore other options within your current location, you can still leave a good impression on the recruiter, even if you cannot relocate. This also shows that you are serious about your career and are open to other opportunities that may arise in the future.

Sample 8

Thank you so much for considering my candidature for the job role in your prestigious organization. However, I will not be able to relocate due to personal reasons. The job profile offered is amazing, and I wish I could have worked with your team.

If there are any opportunities in the future where I could work with your company in the (city's name), I would be more than happy to consider them. It was a pleasure meeting your acquaintance, and I hope to stay in touch with you.

This response shows that even though the candidate cannot relocate, they are still interested in working with the company and open to future opportunities. It also maintains a positive and respectful tone, which can help leave a good impression on the recruiter.

Sample 9

Thank you so much for taking the time out of your busy schedule to meet me and consider my candidature for the post. I am sorry, but I am not considering relocating for personal reasons. I have some family responsibilities here that I need to take care of. However, in the future, I would not mind relocating for a good opportunity and if you would consider my candidature then.

I want to emphasize that I am highly interested in working with your company, and I believe that I can contribute significantly to your organization's growth. If there are any openings in the future, I would be happy to apply and explore the possibility of working with you.

In this response, you politely declined the relocation option and conveyed your interest in working with the company in the future. This shows that you value the opportunity and have a positive attitude toward future possibilities.

Are you sure that you don't want to relocate? It is a great opportunity.

This is a classic recruiter technique to make you reconsider your decision. If you are sure of your decision, here's how to reply.

Sample 10

I appreciate the offer, and the job profile seems interesting. However, I regret to inform you that I won't be able to relocate due to some personal problems that I am currently facing. It is a difficult decision, but I cannot ignore my responsibilities and obligations towards my family and other personal matters.

I understand that my decision may put me at a disadvantage, but I hope you can understand my situation. I am grateful for the opportunity to meet with you and to be considered for the position. I have thoroughly enjoyed our conversation and am impressed with your company's values and work culture.

If any opportunities in the future match my skills and qualifications, I would be delighted to be considered for the role. Once again, thank you for your time and for considering my candidature.

Sample 11

As excited as I am to be joining your prestigious organization, there are certain relocation factors that I wish to discuss with you to ensure a smooth transition and provide an exact date for my joining. As you may know, relocating is a big decision, and I want to make the right choice for myself and my family. I would appreciate it if we could discuss the relocation package your company offers, including details about housing, transportation, and any other relevant information.

I would also like to discuss the timeline for relocation and any possible options for temporary housing until I can find a permanent residence. This will help me plan my move more efficiently and ensure I can join your company as soon as possible.

I understand that these factors may take some time to work out, but I want to ensure that I am fully informed before making any decisions. I appreciate your understanding and cooperation and look forward to hearing from you soon.

Avoid declining the offer with just a No.

It is always better to cite a reason when declining the opportunity to relocate. Otherwise, your recruiter might assume that you are not interested in the job and their company and are taking their time for granted.

Ask for time if you are unsure about relocating.

If you have your doubts about relocating, don't abruptly decline it. Also, if there is confusion about the decision, you can always ask for a day or two to make an informed call. This will ensure the recruiter of your mature and professional attributes.

"Success is not the key to happiness. Happiness is the key to success. If you love what you are doing, you will be successful."

X 2 What Are Your Salary Requirements/ Expectations?

When asked about your salary expectations during an interview, it is important to handle the question tactfully. Here are some ways to respond:

I am looking for a salary that is in line with the industry standards for this position and is commensurate with my experience and qualifications.

I am flexible regarding the salary, as my primary focus is finding a job that aligns with my career goals and offers growth opportunities.

While compensation is an important factor, I am also interested in the overall package offered, such as benefits, bonuses, and opportunities for professional development.

I am open to discussing salary once I have a better understanding of the job responsibilities, the company's expectations, and the benefits package being offered

I am confident that the company will make a fair and competitive offer based on my experience and the position's requirements.

Remember, it's important to balance being honest and tactful when discussing your salary expectations in an interview.

Sample 1

Before I answer that question, I would request more information about this position and its responsibilities. I would also appreciate knowing what is expected of me in this role. I have experience in a similar position over the past few months, which has helped me gauge my worth. However, I understand this position likely entails greater responsibilities, and I believe I would be given important tasks. As for salary or compensation, I am open to negotiation, but I would prefer to learn more about the role before discussing a specific figure.

While being polite, this reflects the speaker's desire to gather more information before making commitments while demonstrating their interest in the position.

Sample 2

This is a challenging question. However, this job position would represent a significant career upgrade for me. I have worked hard for many years to reach my current experience level, and I am eager to bring my skills to your esteemed organization. This opportunity could be a new milestone in my career.

As I understand it, this role would come with greater responsibilities and challenges than I have encountered before. I am excited about tackling these new challenges and expanding my capabilities. However, at this stage, I cannot provide a fixed amount for the role's compensation. I prefer to wait until I have had the opportunity to interact with the manager under whom I will be working so I may get to know more about the team, their challenges, and the expectations from me before settling on a number.

This statement conveys the speaker's excitement for the job opportunity while demonstrating their awareness of its challenges. It also conveys their desire to learn more about the role and its compensation before committing.

Sample 3

I believe it may not be the right time to answer the question regarding my salary expectations. I have yet to understand the work environment and the challenges I would face in this role. Before we can discuss compensation, I would need to delve deeper into the specific responsibilities that I might be undertaking. To accomplish this, I request a managerial interview round to understand the prospective team's requirements better.

Once I have had the opportunity to meet with the Manager and learn more about the nature of the tasks I would be assigned, I will be in a better position to discuss compensation. However, if possible, I would appreciate it if you could give me an idea of the budget for this position. This information would help me to form a more accurate picture of what to expect.

I suggest postponing the salary discussion until I have the necessary information. I am confident that we can arrive at a mutually beneficial salary figure after a more in-depth discussion about the role and its requirements.

This demonstrates the candidate's desire to gather more information before discussing compensation. It also conveys a professional tone and their willingness to negotiate a mutually beneficial agreement once they better understand the role and its requirements.

Sample 4

Before answering this question, I request information regarding the previous employee who held this role. Specifically, I would like to know what the previous employee's qualifications and experience were and what their salary was. This data can help me determine a reasonable compensation figure that aligns with industry standards.

As you know, this position offers many growth opportunities, and I am excited about the prospect of joining your organization. However, at this stage, I hesitate to provide a specific figure for my salary expectations. I prefer a clearer picture of the role's responsibilities and how my skills and experience align with them.

After discussing the role in greater detail, I am confident we can mutually agree on compensation. Therefore, I suggest we postpone this discussion for a day or two to allow further deliberation and debate. Once we have had the opportunity to discuss the role and its requirements, I will be in a better position to provide a more accurate estimate of my salary expectations.

This statement conveys the speaker's desire to make an informed decision based on data and information. It also conveys their willingness to negotiate a fair salary that aligns with their skills and experience while considering the previous employee's compensation.

Sample 5

Thank you for asking me about my salary expectations. It's a difficult question to answer without first understanding the responsibilities and expectations of the role. I am here today because this job opportunity excites me, and I see great potential for career growth within your esteemed organization. I am eager to join a team that values hard work and dedication, and am confident I can contribute to the company's success.

While compensation is an important aspect of any job, my primary focus should be settling into the role and becoming a valuable team member. I must understand the company culture and expectations before we discuss specific compensation figures. I don't want to make a premature guess that may not accurately reflect my worth to the company.

I would like to understand the role in greater detail and take the time to adapt to the work environment before discussing specific salary expectations. I am confident that once we have had the opportunity to discuss the role in greater depth, we can come to a mutually agreeable compensation package.

This conveys the speaker's eagerness to join the team while also emphasizing their desire to take the time to understand the role and adapt to the company culture before discussing specific salary expectations. It also highlights their commitment to becoming a valuable members of the team and contributing to the company's success.

Sample 6

While I appreciate the question, I don't think I can give a satisfactory answer just yet. First and foremost, I want to thank you for considering me for this position. Before we talk about salary, I believe it's important for me to understand the job responsibilities, the work culture, and the expectations from me as an employee. I want to know more about the work hours, location, and project scope. Will there be any opportunities to work on international projects, and if so, will the company sponsor my visa? These are some of the questions that I have in my mind, and once I have a better understanding of the role and its requirements, I can provide a reasonable answer regarding salary expectations. Until then, I would appreciate it if we could put this discussion on hold and focus on the other aspects of the job. Thank you.

Sample 7

I am highly interested in this job because it perfectly aligns with my career goals. I am passionate about developing my skills and honing my talents, and I believe this position will allow me to do so. I look forward to finding a role that will enable me to continue on this path.

This particular company is incredibly appealing to me because it provides an environment conducive to learning and growth. I am eager to take on new challenges and further develop my abilities. The compensation package, while important, is not my top priority. We can reach a mutually beneficial agreement as long as the salary aligns with industry standards and reflects my skills and experience.

My primary goal is to work for a company that values its employees and provides opportunities for personal and professional development. I am excited about the prospect of joining your team and contributing to the company's continued success.

Sample 8

As a fresher, I find it challenging to determine a specific salary expectation. I am still learning to navigate the professional world and don't have much experience negotiating compensation. I am focused on building a successful career. I am eager to expand my knowledge and develop my skills, and I believe that your organization would provide me with ample opportunities to do so. I understand that your company values its employees and offers competitive compensation packages. As a newcomer, I expect a package commensurate with my experience and qualifications. Can you share the average salary range for entry-level positions in your organization? This information will help me better understand the market standards and give me a starting point for negotiation. Ultimately, what matters most to me is the opportunity to learn and grow in a supportive and challenging environment.

Sample 9

My only expectation from this interview is to secure this job position. I believe that my skills and experience align well with the requirements of this organization, and I am excited about the prospect of facing new challenges and opportunities every day.

As for the salary, I am open to negotiating a mutually beneficial figure that aligns with the budget for this position and the responsibilities I will be entrusted with. I understand that the salary package will depend on my role in the organization, and I am willing to work toward the growth and success of the company and my career. I am here to make the most of this opportunity and contribute my best to the growth and success of this esteemed organization.

Sample 10

Being relatively less experienced, I see myself unable to demand any package. I am here for the job as it interests me the most. What money I make from it comes far after. During my internship, I always hoped that a respected organization would have something for me to offer. I feel that the opportunity is in front of me now. It is time to pounce on it. As for the salary, whatever package range is allotted to this job would do for me. I will leave it up to you. Maybe you can respond to this better than me!

While answering this question, you have to be very subtle and patient. Be frank and respond as you wish, but hold your nerves for this. Calm your mind initially. Come up with an answer which can give them a good idea without revealing too much.

“There are people who make things happen, watch things happen, and wonder what happened.”

Y 1 Are You Considering Positions In Other Companies?

This can be a tricky question to answer. On the one hand, you don't want to give the impression that you are not fully committed to this company by mentioning that you are interviewing with other organizations. On the other hand, if you say that you are not considering other positions, it might make you seem like you are not in demand and could hurt your bargaining power in salary negotiations. The best approach is to find common ground between the two answers.

The interviewer is probably asking this question to determine if they have competition in hiring you and to gauge your level of interest in the industry and your commitment to finding employment. If you have other interviews lined up, you can express that you are keeping your options open but prefer this job.

You can still use a similar approach if you don't have many other options. The key is avoiding appearing desperate or having no other options.

- To gauge how quickly they need to move to secure you before another company does
- Assess whether the role you're applying for aligns with your skills and experience
- To ensure that you are genuinely interested in the position
- To understand where you are in the hiring process with other companies
- To determine if their company is your top choice

Here are some examples of how to answer this question:

- I am actively exploring other opportunities, but this position caught my eye because it aligns well with my career goals and interests
- I have some interviews lined up with other companies, but I am most interested in this role because of its reputation and the opportunities it offers
- While I have been exploring other options, I am very excited about this position and would be thrilled to join the team
- I am open-minded about other opportunities, but this position is on my list
- I am committed to finding the right opportunity, and this position aligns perfectly with my career goals and aspirations

Sample 1

I have had the opportunity to interview with two companies in the X and Y industries over the past week. While both of those opportunities are intriguing, I must say that I am particularly drawn to your organization due to my passion for your industry and the impressive work your company has done in recent years. I would be honored to work for you and contribute to your team if everything works out.

Sample 2

No, I haven't been actively looking for a job. However, when my friend [name] mentioned your company and the exciting projects you're working on, I knew I had to apply. I'm not just looking for a job in any company - I'm looking for a challenging and engaging role, and I believe this position would be the perfect fit.

I wasn't actively seeking new opportunities until my friend [name] recommended your company. But as soon as I started reading about your work and the projects in the pipeline, I knew I had to apply. I'm drawn to the type of work you're doing and excited about the prospect of being a part of it.

I wasn't necessarily actively looking for a job, but I always have my ear on the ground for exciting opportunities. When my friend [name] told me about your company and work, I knew it was worth exploring. I'm very selective about the types of companies I apply to - I'm looking for a place where I can be challenged and grow in my career, and I believe your company offers that environment.

Sample 3

I recently started my job search and have found some interesting job postings matching my accounting degree. However, after researching your company and the job description, I am most interested in this position and am very excited about the opportunity to join your team. I appreciate the company's reputation for innovation and the chance to work with a team of industry leaders. I believe my skills and experience align well with the requirements of this position, and I look forward to the possibility of contributing my knowledge to help drive the company's success.

Sample 4

Candidate's specific job role.

While many job opportunities are available in the market, I'm not interested in any position. I'm looking for a role that aligns with my interests and career goals, and I believe that your company and the advertised job fit the bill perfectly. Your business is fascinating, and I'm particularly drawn to the additional responsibilities the position offers in the social media sector. I'm excited about contributing my skills and knowledge to your team.

Candidate's job search strategy.

I've been taking a targeted approach to my job search, focusing on companies and positions that align with my interests and career goals. When I came across your job posting, I knew it was a great fit. Your company's business is interesting, and I'm particularly excited about the opportunity to take on extra tasks in the social media sector. I can bring much value to your team and am eager to explore this opportunity further.

Candidate's interest in social media

I've always been interested in social media, and I'm excited about taking on additional tasks in this area as part of my job. When I saw your job posting, I knew it was the perfect fit. Your company's business is interesting, and I believe I can contribute my skills and knowledge to your team. While there are many opportunities in the market, I'm not interested in any position - I'm looking for a role that aligns with my interests and career goals. I believe your company and the advertised job are a great match.

Sample 5

I'm currently in the process of applying to different job openings. I'm eager to find a new job as soon as possible, but I'm also very selective about the positions I pursue. I always take the time to thoroughly research the company and the job description before deciding whether to apply or accept an interview invitation. However, after researching your company and the role, I am excited to be here today and learn more about the job opportunity. It seems like an excellent fit for my skills and interests, and I believe I could make a meaningful contribution to your team.

Sample 6

I wasn't actively job searching when I came across your posting. I was browsing through job boards and LinkedIn, looking for any unique opportunities that might catch my attention. And when I saw your posting, I was immediately intrigued. While I have applied to a few other jobs, I am only interested in roles that genuinely excite me and align with my career goals.

That being said, I'm excited about the opportunity to learn more about your company and the job role. From what I've seen, it seems like an excellent fit for my skills and experience, and I'm eager to explore it further.

"I can't give you a sure-fire formula for success, but I can give you a formula for failure: try to please everybody all the time."

Y 2 When Can You Start?

Hearing this question about your availability during an interview is an encouraging sign. It indicates that the interviewer is interested in your candidacy and is considering you for the position. Employers often ask about availability to ensure that they can accommodate the candidate's schedule and determine their level of commitment to the job. Therefore, being honest and clear about your availability is important, as it can impact the hiring decision. It is always best to provide a realistic timeline and communicate any scheduling conflicts that may arise. Overall, being asked about availability positively indicates that you are seriously considered for the role.

Sample 1

I am available to start as soon as possible, even from tomorrow. While I have applied to a few other retail companies, I am interested in this position with your company; it would be my first choice. If you decide to allow me to prove my abilities, I am more than ready to start right away.

Please let me know if there is anything else I can do to facilitate a smooth onboarding process.

Sample 2

Indeed, I am flexible and eager to begin working with your company as soon as possible. While this may be a new field, I am confident I can learn quickly and perform well with the proper training and guidance. I understand there will be an orientation and training period, and I welcome this opportunity to develop my skills and knowledge within the company's unique environment.

Taking the time to learn and understand the role fully will benefit me and the company in the long run. I want to ensure I provide the highest quality work possible and meet all expectations. So, I am willing to invest the necessary time and effort to ensure that I can perform the job responsibilities to the best of my ability.

That being said, I am ready to start as soon as you need me to, and I am excited about the opportunity to begin working with your team.

Sample 3

I am currently employed under a contract with my current employer, and as per the terms of my agreement, I must serve a notice period of two months after submitting my resignation letter. While I understand the importance of fulfilling my contractual obligations, I also want to ensure a smooth transition for my current employer and the company I may join.

I have established a good rapport with the HR team and my superior at my current workplace. I have informed them about my job search and the potential of securing a new opportunity. Given my positive relationship with them, I believe they would consider allowing me to leave earlier than the two-month notice period if it aligns with their business needs.

If you decide to offer me the position, I will discuss this matter with my current employer and ensure a seamless transition. I value professionalism and want to maintain a positive relationship with my current employer.

Sample 4

I appreciate your interest in having me start as soon as possible. However, I want to be responsible and considerate of my current employer and ensure a smooth transition for my replacement. Therefore, while I could start tomorrow, I believe it would be more appropriate to give my current employer ample notice and time to find a suitable replacement.

In accordance with my employment contract, I need to provide at least two weeks' notice before resigning. Additionally, I feel it's important to train my successor and help them to take over my existing projects so that there is no disruption to the company's workflow.

I value my time with my present employer and have learned a great deal from my experience there. I want to leave on good terms and maintain a positive relationship with them. Therefore, I estimate that I will need about two to three weeks to properly transition out of my current role and start with your company with a clear conscience and focus on contributing to your organization to the best of my abilities.

Sample 5

This is my first time applying for a job, and I'm excited about the opportunities that have come my way. I haven't signed any employment contract, so I have the flexibility to consider different options. Recently, I was invited to interview for a position in two other companies, and I accepted the invitation. I feel that it's important to explore different opportunities before making a final decision.

However, I have to say that I was particularly impressed with the interview I had with you. Your business values align with mine, and your company has an exceptional reputation. I am inclined to work for you, and I would be thrilled to have the opportunity to join your team.

After my last interview, which takes place in two days, I will have a better idea of my options. I can start the training immediately if I decide to work for you. I hope you can appreciate my honesty and openness throughout this process. I am excited about possibly working with your company and contributing to your team.

Sample 6

I have been preparing for this job opportunity for a long time, and I am excited to start working in a role that aligns with my career goals and passions. I have done thorough research on your company and its values, and I am impressed with the innovative work culture and opportunities for growth that you offer.

Furthermore, I understand that sometimes starting immediately may not be feasible for certain reasons. If that is the case, I am open to discussing the timeline and finding a mutually suitable start date. However, if I can begin my employment sooner, I am available and excited to do so.

Ultimately, my goal is to contribute my skills and experience to your team and make a positive impact in the role. I am committed to being a reliable and dedicated employee and look forward to working with you.

"The master has failed more times than the beginner has even tried."

Z1 Do You Want To Tell Us Anything Else About Yourself?

The more closely your credentials match the job requirements, the better your chances of getting an offer. Emphasize more about your strong interest in the job and in working for the organization. Start your answer with a summary of some of the key strengths you have already shared. This will help the interviewer remember why you are a strong candidate. Add one or two items from your list that haven't been covered. These can be skills or abilities you have not yet mentioned. Make sure whatever you say is relevant to the position.

Sample 1

I haven't had the opportunity to discuss my sales skills with you. Being persuasive has been a valuable asset in my prior position. As we have already covered many of my strengths, including writing, presentation, and computer skills, I would like to add an example of my salesmanship. For instance, during my previous job, I convinced seven local businesses to sponsor the charity run I organized for my organization. In addition, during my public relations internship, I successfully placed several stories in local media about a client, demonstrating my ability to communicate effectively and influence others.

Sample 2

I want to share that I am working on improving my skills and knowledge in marketing. Although we have already discussed my previous work experiences, I believe it is important to mention that I am currently taking a course with Google Ads to enhance my abilities in creating and delivering ads to a target audience. The course also covers analyzing and interpreting the ads' data to determine their effectiveness. I am confident that this additional knowledge will enable me to contribute even more to the marketing department and help the company achieve its goals.

Sample 3

One crucial skill I would like to bring to your attention is my proficiency in web design. I recently had the opportunity to showcase this skill during an internship at Anytech Public Relations. During the internship, I was crucial in designing and developing a new website for one of their clients. I utilized my knowledge of web design platforms such as Squarespace, WordPress, Webflow, and Wix to create a visually appealing and user-friendly website.

While we have already touched upon my other key strengths, such as my communication skills, ability to collaborate across departments, and experience in public relations, I believe that my web design skills will also be valuable to your company. The client for whom I designed the website was very pleased with the result and even sent a letter to our CEO praising my skills. I am excited to bring my web design expertise to your company and contribute to its success.

Sample 4

I want to share more about my sales experience with you. As previously discussed, I have strong problem-solving skills and am a collaborative team player committed to efficiently addressing customer issues.

In my previous role, I provided customer service by speaking with customers to understand their needs. By building rapport with them, I could identify which of the company's products or services would best fit them. In addition to providing excellent customer service, I successfully sold products and services to customers.

My sales experience, strong communication skills, and ability to work well with others make me an ideal candidate for this position. I am confident that I would be able to contribute to your team's success and help drive sales for your company.

Sample 5

I have nine years of teaching experience, including two years in an administrative role. As we discussed, my communication skills have been honed through my experience working with students, parents, and fellow educators to achieve academic and personal goals. Additionally, I have a strong record of facilitating positive and productive relationships between students of diverse backgrounds.

One aspect of my experience we haven't touched on is my work leading after-school programs. At my previous school, I oversaw the school newspaper, which had a staff of thirty students, and the literary journal, which had twelve teams. This involved managing deadlines, assigning tasks, and guiding students in their creative and journalistic pursuits. This experience demonstrates my ability to lead and motivate a team and my dedication to fostering student engagement beyond the classroom.

Finally, I want to emphasize my enthusiasm for this opportunity. I am excited about the prospect of contributing to your school's community and making a meaningful impact on student lives.

Sample 6

It is important to mention my post-graduate goals and some of the experiences that led me to pursue a master's degree in accounting. My desire to pursue a career in accounting stems from my love for numbers and interest in analyzing financial statements. After completing my bachelor's degree in finance, I gained valuable experience working as an intern at a local accounting firm. This experience allowed me to gain a deeper understanding of the accounting field and helped me develop a strong foundation in accounting principles.

I am excited about the master's program in accounting that I am pursuing because I believe it will further enhance my knowledge and skills in this field. I am particularly interested in learning more about tax accounting and how to navigate complex tax laws.

I am eager to apply the knowledge and skills I have gained from my academic and professional experience to this position. My passion for accounting, attention to detail, and strong work ethic make me an excellent fit for this job. I am grateful for the opportunity to be considered for this position and am excited about possibly joining your team.

Sample 7

I am developing another skill to make me an even more effective employee. I am currently enrolled in a computer programming course and am learning SQL and Java.

We have discussed many of my skills, abilities, and experiences that make me a strong candidate, including my experience working with clients and my written and oral communication skills. I am incredibly passionate about this job opportunity and believe in my skills.

Sample 8

I mentioned my experience leading a graphic design team for a major redesign project during our conversation. However, I failed to mention my freelance work and the different types of graphic design projects that I have undertaken for various clients.

Apart from the redesign project, I have worked on other design projects such as rebranding, logo design, and signage for major local events. These tasks required me to work closely with clients to understand their vision and create designs that effectively captured their brand identity and message.

My experience working with clients and ability to take on various graphic design tasks would make me a strong candidate for this position. I'm passionate about design and constantly seek new ways to improve my skills and stay up-to-date with industry trends.

"I attribute my success to this: I never gave or took any excuse."

Z 2 Do You Have Any Questions For Us?

Asking thoughtful and relevant questions during an interview can demonstrate your engagement and interest in the company and help you better understand its goals and priorities. You can reflect on earlier moments in the interview to show that you were paying attention and thinking about the topics discussed. For example, you could ask for more details about a project or initiative mentioned earlier or seek clarification on a raised point.

Another way to ask relevant questions is to build off recent news or developments in the company or its market. For example, you could ask about the company's strategy for entering a new market or how they plan to adapt to changes in the industry. This not only shows that you have done your research but also that you are forward-thinking and interested in the company's plans.

Asking thoughtful and relevant questions during an interview can help you make a positive impression and gain valuable insights into the company's goals and priorities.

Sample 1

Can you please tell me the next steps in the hiring process? Additionally, I came across an online interview where your CEO mentioned that your company is interested in working with voice recognition technology. I find that very intriguing. Will this role involve any work related to such projects?

Sample 2

Your job advertisement mentioned that you seek someone with talent in inbound sales. I have three years of experience as a sales associate at a local store in my area, where I honed my ability to approach customers and ask the right questions to understand their needs. I also learned how to handle demanding customers and solve crises while remaining persistent without being pushy. I believe these skills would make me an asset to any sales team.

I am curious; could you tell me more about the team I would be joining? How many people are currently on the team?

Sample 3

I have been following your company's success for some time now, and I know you have a great software development team. This would be the perfect environment for me to apply the skills I acquired during my internship and Master's degree. I regularly checked your careers page, and when I saw this job ad, I knew it was finally time to take the leap. With my experience in web development and a keen interest in the projects mentioned in the job ad (one of which was the subject of my thesis), I genuinely believe that I am an excellent fit for this position and can continue to grow in your workplace. Are there any qualifications you feel that I am missing?

Sample 4

First, the job description was well-written and gave me a good idea of the role. Second, I liked that this accounting role involves collaboration with others. I love accounting, but I don't want to sit at my desk to look at numbers all day – I want to have the chance to work as part of a team where we can exchange opinions and knowledge of new accounting methods and organize the company accounting department in the best way possible. What would you want me to achieve in my first two months if I were hired for this role?

Sample 5

I have the requisite skills to make your risk worth it. Chatting less and letting my work do the talking is my motto. In the past, whatever project was assigned to me was delivered on time and at par with all the quality standards. What are your concerns about my candidacy?

Questions could include the role:

- Can you share more about the day-to-day responsibilities of this role? How would you describe the pace of a typical day?
- What would you want me to achieve in my first two months if I were hired for this role?
- What mechanisms are in place for performance reviews, and when would I receive my first formal evaluation?
- In your opinion, what is the most critical indicator of success in this role?

Questions could include about the company or interviewer

- How would you describe the management style of the organization?
- What's something that makes you happy about coming to work each day?
- How long have you been at the company?
- Can you talk about company culture?
- What is the greatest challenge facing the company?
- What are the company's goals for the upcoming year?

Questions could include about yourself.

- What are your concerns about my candidacy?
- Are there any qualifications that you think I'm missing?

If your question makes them uncomfortable even for a second, you may have undone all your hard work. It raises questions about what you'd be like to work with and whether you take the needs of others into account. Or it simply leaves a question about your judgment when working for them.

Questions arising from the discussion during the interview are often the best. They show you were actively listening, are interested, and can follow up on such things as you might in an actual job.

"A successful man can lay a firm foundation with the bricks others have thrown at him."

Steer The Interview: Do's And Don't's

Many candidates go to interviews thinking they are there for only one reason: to answer the questions. Nothing could be further from the truth. Yes, you are going to the interview for one reason only: to sell the interviewer on the fact that you are the best person for the job. You will do this by giving terrific answers to the interviewer's questions, asking great questions about the company and the position, and telling the interviewer the things about yourself that you want them to know. Let's say you went to an automobile showroom knowing just a little about a particular car. You are approached by a pleasant salesman who answers your questions but doesn't volunteer any information and asks no questions of you. Do you think you'd end up buying a car from him? Most candidates approach the job interview like this hapless salesman. They are prepared to answer questions but hesitate to volunteer information unless it's asked for, even if that information concerns some of their key talents or strengths.

Do not miss the opportunity to sell yourself. The fact that a customer walked into the showroom should motivate that car salesman to do his best. Likewise, the fact that you have an interview call gives you a chance to sell yourself. Please don't blow it up because the interviewers don't ask the questions you expected. Anyway, find a way to give your answer.

Many less-experienced interviewers tend to talk too much. In those situations, you must take charge and ask questions constantly. If the interviewer has been speaking nonstop for 10 minutes when he says, We've increased sales 20 percent every year for the past decade, politely interrupt with a question like, That's very impressive in a mature industry like yours. How has the company maintained such growth? At the opposite extreme is the interviewer, who will let the poor candidate ramble on and on in answer to a single question because he has so few others to ask. If you face such a situation, watch how the interviewer reacts to your monologue. If he exhibits what seems to be a negative response—crossing his arms across his chest, sitting bolt upright in his chair, fidgeting, tapping his fingers on the desk, shuffling papers, change the subject, or ask him a question. You are not getting anywhere by continuing to flap your gums.

Please don't make the mistake of talking faster once you notice his discomfort. You may think this will help you get to whatever the interviewer wants to hear more quickly. It's more likely that he wants to listen to his voice for a minute or two!

Make sure you maintain eye contact and answer questions clearly and concisely. It's okay to take a moment to think before answering a question, but try not to pause for too long. Finally, follow up with the interviewer after the interview to thank them for their time and express your continued interest in the role.

Interview Checklist

Do's

A day before the interview

You need to prepare, and there's no reason to worry. To help, here are things you should do the night before an interview.

- Ensure you're not scrambling to come up with something appropriate in the morning. Select the dress you will wear and ensure it is clean, well-ironed, and without missing buttons. Plus, ensure your shoes match and have a matching pair of socks. Ensure that your outfits suit the post for which you are applying
- If you wear a turban, ensure it matches your outfit and is neatly tied

Collect all your certificates, mark–sheets, and other relevant papers and file them sequentially in a neat folder. Use Google Maps to ensure you know the route, and check any emails from the company for information on transit, parking, and confusing entrances. If you're interviewing at a big building or company, plan on spending five to 10 minutes dealing with security

- Go through your CV, mark sheets, and certificates, and mentally prepare to answer questions on your CV
- Before an interview, you should understand the company's products and services and any recent developments and news. You should also know your interviewers' names, titles, and departments. Do a

quick Google search and a little LinkedIn stalking to get some background on their interests and what they might be working on

- This pre-interview research will inform your answers and help you break the ice and make a connection
- Every interview has a different feel, but you can still practice. The easiest way to do that is to review some of the most common interview questions, which will help you feel prepared and confident
- Jot down all the details: who you're meeting with and their titles, a couple of past work accomplishments or stories you want to bring up, and the questions you want to ask at the end. Preparing like this can be a lifesaver when you're moments away from meeting the hiring manager and blanking on their name
- Brush up your general knowledge, and collect essential facts on current events, especially about your state
- Set your alarm and avoid the snooze button to ensure you have the necessary time
- Before the interview, a whole night's sleep is required to remain fit and fresh during the day. Sleep is your secret weapon for a job interview, ensuring you're charming and lively. To get some quality shut-eye, turn off your TV, and put down the mobile phone! Social media will still be there after your interview the next day

On the day of the interview

- Avoid rushing. Set the alarm for the time you have to leave. Arrive at least 10–15 minutes early
- Bring the supplies you prepared the night before your interview
- Eat a healthy breakfast. Don't let a gurgling stomach affect your performance
- Turn off all mobile devices. Put away your phone

- Relax
- Be friendly to everyone. Be considerate and polite to all staff members. You never know who will provide input for a hiring decision
- Avoid any scents or jewelry that may be distracting to the employer
- Do not smoke right before your interview
- Discard any chewing gum or breathe mints before your interview
- Ask questions
- Listen
- Be enthusiastic and smile!

During the interview

- Smile first and then smile often. It's the best defense against nervousness
- Maintain eye contact at all times to convey confidence
- Modulate your tone and speaking style, and practice your pitch and pace at home often.
- Be natural with facial expressions, avoid nervous gestures, and stay calm, composed, and pleasant
- Demonstrate energy by keeping an upright posture, and make sure you don't slump or slouch
- Speak in a clear voice and make sure each word is audible
- Be a good listener so that you know what is being asked. If you cannot understand any question, request the members to repeat it, saying, I beg your pardon. Don't start your answer until you have understood what is being asked

- Give a well-thought-out, balanced answer and be prompt so the interviewers can ask as many questions as they like. You have to help them make a proper judgment
- When replying to a question asked by any particular member, look at him directly, and address your answer to him
- Maintain a pleasant expression throughout. It would be best not to look ill, at ease, or anxious
- Suppose you are discussing a serious topic. You cannot continue smiling when a grave or tragic situation is concerned
- If the chairman or any member appreciates your discussion or your point, take the opportunity to thank him for the compliment immediately
- Be relaxed throughout without showing any signs of anxiety. Try to give the impression of being an ambitious young man willing to take on any challenge
- Look at all the members individually while addressing your answers, and do not concentrate all the time on the chairman or any particular board member

After the interview

- After the interview, when asked to leave, get up, and thank all the members present
- If the Chairman extends his hand, take the opportunity to shake hands firmly and confidently
- Leave the chair calmly and put it back in its proper position. Turn to leave, portraying an upright bearing
- Walk confidently, giving the impression of having achieved the desired goal
- Don't turn back to look at the members

- Don't forget the interview board observes your manners of leaving the hall
- Don't forget to close the door after you
- Send a thank you note within 24 hours of the interview
- If you do not hear from the employer after the hiring timeline, they initially indicated follow-up professionally and only once
- Evaluate your performance: Did any questions stump you? Now is the time to improve your answers for the next interview
- After a first-round interview, you may be called back for additional rounds of interviews depending on the employer's process
- If a job offer is provided on the spot, which is uncommon, it is appropriate to thank the employer and to tell them that you need more time to consider the opportunity

DON'TS

On the day of the interview

- Don't eat a heavy breakfast on the day of your interview, as it might make you feel uncomfortable or heavy

During the interview

- Don't forget to close the door after you have entered the interview hall
- Don't forget to ask permission before coming in
- Don't forget a timely salutation when you have reached the table of the Interviewer. Greet them according to the time
- Don't sit down on your own. Wait for the chairman's instructions to take a seat
- Don't start on your own. Let the Interviewer initiate the proceeding

- Don't speak too fast. Let every word you say to be clear and audible to all the members
- Don't make artificial or excessive gesticulation. Try to be as normal and relaxed as possible
- Don't be emotional on any particular point to win the favor of the interview board
- Don't interrupt the others. Let the chairman or the interviewers finish speaking. You may request that he repeat it if you have not followed it
- Don't enter into any argument with the Interviewer or any member of the Board
- Don't try to avoid questions. If two or more members have put their questions consecutively, reply to each one in the same order
- Don't give confusing answers. If you are unsure of something, be frank and politely say, Sir, I am not aware of such a thing or Sir, I am sorry I do not know
- Don't fiddle around with your buttons, hair, or anything else, as it shows nervousness
- Don't change your stand. Be consistent in the line of argument you have chosen. Do not give self–contradictory or conflicting answers
- Don't readily agree with everything the interviewer says if you have valid arguments to support your point of view. In case of disagreement, be polite and say, I beg to differ sir, and try to convince him of your point of view
- Don't try to gain the favor of the Interviewer /chairman or any of the members by giving a biased opinion, which you think, might please him. This will not show your maturity or integrity
- Don't enter into any political controversy. Never try to gain the favor of the interviewers by speaking against or in favor of any particular community

- While arguing a point, don't give up until the interviewer changes the topic
- Don't miss the opportunity to compliment the interviewer

After the interview

Just because you might feel like you've nailed a job interview doesn't mean you can call off the search. A great interview is only one factor in finding the right candidate.

- The hiring process takes a lot longer than most job seekers care to admit. This can cause a range of emotions for a job seeker, including insecurity, worry, and even anger. Keep calm, and don't make the mistake of reaching out too soon to your potential employer
- Even if your interview experience was less than enjoyable, contacting your potential employer is essential. Take the necessary steps to show your gratitude for the opportunity
- Nothing will scare a potential employer away like an overly aggressive job seeker. Use tact and respect in your approach to your post-interview steps. A simple thank you note and an email will be enough to express your gratitude. Phone calls and constant emails aren't necessary

"You miss 100% of the shots you don't take."

www.ingramcontent.com/pod-product-compliance
Ingram Content Group UK Ltd.
Pitfield, Milton Keynes, MK11 3LW, UK
UKHW041858190726
13854UKWH00002B/966

9 798890 267580